P. A. Stuart

The Inside Guide to

The iPad

For Seniors

2nd Edition

Covers up to the Pro and the iOS 9 operating system

The Inside Guide to the iPad for Seniors

Published by IGT Publishing

ISBN-13: 978-0993475221
ISBN-10: 0993475221

Contents

Chapter 1 – Controlling Your iPad

Chapter 2 – iPad Elements & Features

Chapter 3 – The Keyboard

Chapter 4 – Setting Up Your iPad

Chapter 5 – Apps

Chapter 6 – Getting Online

Chapter 7 – Communicating

Chapter 8 – Organization

Chapter 9 – Entertainment

Chapter 10 – Reading

Chapter 11 – Security

Chapter 12 – iCloud & Related Services

Chapter 13 – Useful Third-Party Apps

Chapter 14 – Troubleshooting & Maintenance

Index

CHAPTER 1

Controlling Your iPad

Apple's iPad is not only compact and stylish, it is constructed to a very high standard. It also runs an operating system, iOS, that is renowned for its high levels of security. As a result, you are extremely unlikely to get a virus or malware on your iPad.

An incredibly useful tablet, the iPad has something to offer all age groups. However, some aspects of the device make it particularly useful for the older generation as we'll see.

In this opening chapter, we introduce you to the iPad, its controls and the iOS operating system that underpins it.

Introduction

Despite its sleek look and compact dimensions, the iPad is a actually quite a powerhouse as portable computing devices go. It may not have the 'grunt' of a desktop computer or laptop but it is, nevertheless, capable of a wide range of functions. These include:

Communication
The iPad lets you send/receive email, text messages, use social media, and make video calls. You can also use it as a telephone if it is a cellular model.

Browsing the Internet
One of the iPad's best features is that you can access and browse the Internet wherever you happen to be (assuming you are within range of a network). Because it is not physically connected to anything, the Internet can be accessed, quite literally, from anywhere.

Organization
The iPad provides a number of apps that help you to organize and manage your life. These include a calendar, an address book, reminders, and notes.

Entertainment
Your iPad is an entertainment center. Not only can you play games on it, you can watch TV and movies, listen to music, and read books.

Photography
While it is no match for a dedicated camera, the iPad is still capable of taking decent pictures. The large screen is also ideal for viewing them.

Work
There are many apps available in the App Store which enable you to word-process, create spreadsheets and presentations, scan, print, and more.

Being so light, the iPad is extremely portable. It also comes with a rechargeable battery that provides approximately 10 hours of power, and a high resolution Retina touchscreen display.

iPad Models

iPads are available in a range of models. Currently, these are the Pro, Air 2, Air, Mini 4 and the Mini 2.

iPad Pro
Released in late 2015, the Pro is the most recent iPad. This is the largest model with dimensions of 12 x 8.6 x .27 inches, and a diagonal screen size of 12.9 inches. The Pro is the most powerful and thus capable of the iPads. It is also the most expensive, and is intended for business users who will appreciate the large screen and extra power that will let them multitask and use the latest applications. Additionally, there is a range of accessories for it that include the Apple Pencil (a digital stylus pen that works as an input device), and a Smart Keyboard.

iPad Air 2
The premier iPad until being succeeded by the Pro, the Air 2 is still a highly capable device. It is the next largest of the iPads with dimensions of 9.4 x 6.6 x .24 inches, and a diagonal screen size of 9.7 inches. It is less powerful than the Pro due to its less capable A8X processor (the Pro has a A9X).

iPad Air
The iPad Air was replaced by the Air 2 and is getting a bit long in the tooth now. That said, it still provides everything the vast majority of people require from a tablet. Its main disadvantage is its A7 processor that is beginning to struggle with the latest apps, which are demanding ever more processing power.

iPad Mini 4
Both the Air and Air 2 have mini, scaled down, versions. The Air 2's is the Mini 4. This iPad has dimensions of 8 x 5.3 x .24 inches, and a diagonal screen size of 7.9 inches. The only other difference of note is that it costs less.

iPad Mini 2
This iPad is the mini version of the Air. It's dimensions are 7.7 x 5.3 x .29 inches, and has a diagonal screen size of 7.9 inches. As with the Mini 4, it has the same capabilities as it's larger cousin, the Air, while costing less.

All the iPads come with two cameras – a main rear-facing iSight camera and a front-facing FaceTime HD camera. The iSight supplied with the Pro, Air 2 and Mini 4 takes 8 MP photos while the Air and the Mini 2 take 5 MP photos.

All iPad models are available in Wi-Fi only and Wi-Fi/cellular versions. The former enables the iPad to connect to the Internet via Wi-Fi. The latter can connect not only via Wi-Fi but also via mobile networks.

With regard to storage, the iPads are available in capacities of 16 GB, 32 GB, 64 GB and 128 GB – fairly obviously, the larger the better.

Terminology

Before we go any further, it may be helpful to give a brief explanation of some of the terminology you're going to encounter in this book.

App
The word app is short for application. Apps are software programs installed on the iPad that enable it to do things. For example, the Mail app lets you send/receive email and the Safari app lets you browse the Internet.

Apple ID
This is an account that users set up with Apple (makers of the iPad). With it, you can make purchases from the App, iTunes, and iBook Stores. It can also be used to access Apple services such as iCloud and Photo Library.

Synchronization
Also known as syncing, synchronization is where data is shared between two computing devices via a third-party computer. Any changes made to synced data on device A are automatically sent to the third-party computer and then on to device B (and vice versa). The data is thus synchronized between all three devices, i.e. kept the same. The term is also used to describe the transfer of data, e.g. pictures, from a user's computer to their iPad.

Cloud/Cloud Computing/iCloud
The Cloud is the term used for a third-party computer (as mentioned above) that is used for data storage and synchronization. The process of saving and sending data to and from the Cloud is known as Cloud Computing.

iCloud is Apple's version of the Cloud and offers various related services such as iCloud Drive, contact synchronization, Find My iPhone, iTunes Match, etc.

iOS
All computing devices need an operating system that runs in the background to provide a platform for the programs, or apps. iOS is the iPad's operating system and is currently at version 9; hence iOS 9.

iTunes
iTunes is a computer program made by Apple that users employ to manage their various Apple devices. For example, it can be used to upload music, video and e-books from a PC to the iPad. It can also create and restore iPad backups.

Lightening Connector
Lightning is the name Apple gives to the connection port used to connect its most recent iPhone, iPod Touch and iPad models to the power supply for charging, or to a computer for charging and/or synchronization.

Bluetooth
Bluetooth is a low-power wireless network technology that works over short distances. It is built into millions of consumer products.

Controls

Your iPad initiation begins with the power button. Situated at the top-right of the device, this control actually serves two functions:

● On/Off switch

● Wake/Sleep switch

Power button

On/Off Switch

To switch your iPad on, press the button and hold it down until you see a white screen with the Apple logo. Release the button and wait for the Home screen to appear. When it does, your iPad is ready to use.

To switch your iPad off, press and hold the button down until you see the 'slide to power off' slider.

slide to power off

Place a finger on the slider and move it all the way to the right. A few seconds later the iPad will shut down. If you change your mind about switching off just press the Cancel button at the bottom of the screen.

Typically, you'll want to switch the device off to conserve battery power or when it won't be in use for a while. Usually though, it's left on Standby.

Wake/Sleep Switch

When the iPad is in use, it can be switched to Sleep mode (also known as Standby mode) by pressing the power button once. This cuts the power to the touchscreen thus turning it off (you'll see it go black). As a result, the power used by the device drops considerably.

Note that any apps that are running when the device is put to sleep continue to run. For example, if your email app is running, the device will still receive incoming emails. Sleep mode also prevents accidental inputs (taps) from inadvertently triggering functions on the device. This also helps to reduce power consumption.

Generally speaking then, putting your iPad to sleep whenever it is not in use is the way to go. There is, however, one exception to this rule and it applies to owners of cellular equipped iPads who travel abroad. Be aware that even in Sleep mode, the iPad will continually attempt to connect to any available network. If you are aren't using a suitable international data plan, this can result in high data roaming charges.

Therefore, when overseas, make sure you have disabled 'Cellular Data' and 'Data Roaming' in Network Settings in the Settings app. Alternatively, turn the iPad off when not in use. Sleep mode is not a good option in this situation.

Volume Controls

To control the volume on your iPad, the Pro, Air 2, and Mini 4 models provide the two controls shown below:

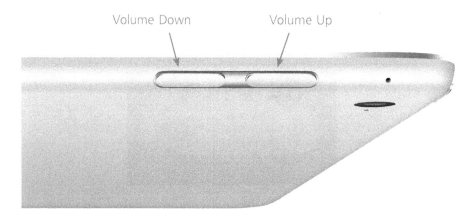

Volume Down   Volume Up

Press either of the switches and you'll see a speaker window (shown overleaf) appear on the screen with a volume level bar at the bottom.

- Press the Volume Up switch repeatedly to increase the volume in steps

- Hold the Volume Up switch down for maximum volume

- Press the Volume Down switch repeatedly to decrease the volume in steps

- Hold the Volume Down switch down to mute the iPad

Screen Rotation Lock
With the Air and Mini 2 iPad models, just above the volume controls is a small switch known as the Side switch. The purpose of this switch is to lock the iPad in either Portrait or Landscape mode to prevent it changing when the orientation of the device is altered.

With the newer Pro, Air 2 and Mini 4 iPad models, the switch has been removed and the function is carried out with the Control Center (see pages 24-25) as we explain below:

1. Hold the iPad in the desired orientation – Portrait or Landscape

2. Swipe up from the bottom of the screen to open the Control Center

3. Tap the Orientation button to lock the iPad in the required orientation

Having the screen orientation locked can be useful in certain situations. Of course there are times, such as when browsing the Internet, that having it off is also desirable. Whichever, your iPad lets you choose for yourself.

cont'd

Home Button

Now we come to one of the main features of your iPad – the Home button. This is located at the front of the device at the bottom.

Home button

The control you'll probably use the most, the Home button provides a number of functions:

- If your iPad is a Pro, Air 2 or Mini 4 model, there will be a biometric fingerprint scanner built-in to the button. This recognizes your fingerprint and will automatically unlock the iPad without the need for a passcode to be entered. It can also be used to authorize purchases from the iTunes Store, the App Store, and the iBooks Store

- When your iPad is in Standby mode, pressing the Home button wakes the device and displays the Lock screen

- Wherever you are in the iPad, or whatever you are doing, pressing the Home button immediately takes you to the Home screen

- If you have several home screens and are not on the main one, you will be switched to it

- Pressing and holding the Home button down activates the iPad's voice recognition feature, Siri (assuming it has been enabled). Siri allows you to control many of the iPad's functions with voice commands.

- If you have the touchscreen turned off while playing a track with the Music app, pressing the Home button will bring up the music controls allowing you to pause, play, adjust the volume, etc. You won't be able to select which tracks to play in this view though

- Double-pressing the Home button gives you access to the iPad's multitasking interface. This shows all apps that are open and allows you to quickly switch between them. It also lets you shut the apps down by swiping upwards on the app in question. We'll see more on this feature later on

Hardware Features

So far we've covered your iPad's physical controls. Let's see what other hardware features it offers.

Looking at the bottom edge of the device, you'll see three things:

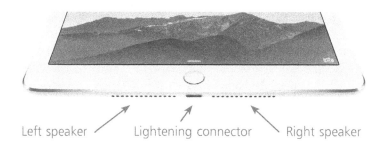

Left speaker   Lightening connector   Right speaker

At the left and right are two loudspeakers (on all models apart from the Pro, which has four) that give a stereo effect as long as the device is held in Portrait mode. Between the loudspeakers is a Lightning connector that you will use to charge the iPad, and also to connect it to a computer or laptop in order to use Apple's iTunes software.

Turn your attention to the top-rear of your iPad and you'll see a headphone jack, dual microphones, and a camera lens.

Microphones   Headphone jack

Camera

The 3.5mm headphone jack is where you connect a set of headphones to listen to the audio output of your iPad.

The dual microphones enable your iPad to capture clear sound and help to reduce background noise during FaceTime calls.

At the top-right of the iPad is the main camera – this takes 8 megapixel pictures (5 megapixels with the older Air and Mini 2 models) of reasonable quality. At the front of the iPad, at the top, is another camera – this is a lower quality 1.2 megapixel affair (all models) that is intended for making FaceTime video calls, taking 'selfies' and the like.

The iOS Operating System

iOS is the name given to the operating system used on the various mobile Apple devices – the iPad, iPhone and the iPod Touch. iOS 9 is the latest version and is the one covered in this book.

One of the best things about iOS is its security. The chances of getting a virus or malware when using an Apple device are much less than with devices that run Google's Android or Microsoft's Windows. Apple's 'walled garden' App Store – where applications are fully vetted before being made available to customers – has prevented widespread infection of iOS devices. This gives users confidence that they won't be compromizing their iPad by downloading apps and music, etc.

Another of its great features is the way it links, or synchronizes, with other Apple devices. iOS 9 and OS X El Capitan (the latest operating system used on Apple Macs) are effectively joined at the hip with the Handoff feature that lets you pick up where you left off between devices. For example, you can start a project or email message on an iPad or iPhone and then finish the task on a Mac.

Similarly, with iCloud Drive you can store your PDFs, presentations, spreadsheets, images and any other kind of document in iCloud and access them from your iPhone, iPad, iPod Touch, Mac or personal computer.

iOS 9 introduces a number of new features, which include a News app (sure to prove popular), multi-app multitasking that lets you run apps side-by-side together with the ability to quickly switch between them, and picture-in-picture that lets you watch videos in a small window while working in another app.

There are also many improvements to existing features, such as making the Siri and Search functions broader and more proactive, a complete rebuild of the popular Notes app, and the addition of transit and other features to Maps. There are also enhancements to the keyboard, improved performance and battery life, and a tightening up of security and privacy features.

You should be aware that while most iPads are compatible with iOS 9, not all of them will be able to support the more powerful features introduced in iOS 9. For example, Split View (pages 22-23) will only work on the Pro, Air 2 and Mini 4. Furthermore, some features found in iOS 9 for iPhones will not be available on iPads and vice versa.

The Spotlight search function now gives you suggestions from Wikipedia, places nearby, trending news and more. It's also smart enough to recognize context and location, and thus offer you the most relevant information.

CHAPTER 2

iPad Elements & Features

In Chapter Two, we take a look at the main elements of your iPad. These include the various screens, all of which provide a specific function plus shortcuts to other functions.

You will learn how to use finger movements with the iPad's touchscreen – these enable you to operate and control the device. An important iPad feature is Notifications, which advises you of events with messages and alerts – we show you how to set this up.

You'll also learn how to find things on your iPad with the Spotlight Search tool, and access commonly used functions with the Control Center.

Home Screen

Once you have completed the setup wizard (see Chapter 4), you will be taken to the Home screen as shown below. This has three sections:

- Status bar
- Main screen
- Dock bar

Status bar

Main screen

Dock bar

cont'd

The Status Bar
Situated right at the top of the screen is a very narrow bar, which is called the Status Bar. The bar itself is transparent but the information it displays is visible in white text and can include any of the following:

- **Airplane mode** – an airplane icon appears at the far-left of the Status bar when Airplane mode is selected

- **Network connection** – displayed at the far-left, this icon indicates that you're connected to a network – Wi-Fi for example

- **Activity** – this icon appears when a task is in progress

- **Time** – the current time is displayed right in the middle of the Status bar

- **Rotation lock** – when present, this indicates that the screen orientation is locked

- **Battery** – displayed at the far-right, the battery icon shows the level of charge in the battery. You also see it in figures, e.g. 40%

The above are just some of the features and functions that use the Status bar.

The Main Screen
The main part of the screen is reserved for the iPad's apps and has room for 20. If the device has more than 20 installed apps, the extra ones are placed on a second home screen. When this screen is fully populated as well, a third home screen is created and so on.

Each home screen is represented by a small white dot above the middle of the Dock bar. To navigate between the screens, just swipe left and right. Pressing the Home button takes you to the first home screen.

The Dock Bar
The Dock bar is a section of the screen reserved for the user's favorite apps. It is present at the bottom of all the iPad's home screens and so the favorite apps are always instantly accessible.

By default, the Dock bar is populated with four apps but you can add two more to make a total of six. You can also replace the default apps with apps of your own choice as we'll see later.

Screen Orientation
You can view the Home screen in either Portrait or Landscape mode – simply rotate the iPad to switch between the two. If you want to use one mode permanently, you can set this up as we explained on page 13.

The Touchscreen

You should by now be familiar with the physical aspects of your iPad. So it's time to see what goes on inside the device and, to do this, you need to know how to operate the touchscreen.

This is a quite amazing part of the iPad and it is controlled by nothing more than your finger or, in some cases, fingers.

You can create folders, scroll through lists, zoom in and zoom out, drag and drop items, and type messages. No external hardware is required – just the following finger movements, or gestures as they are known:

- **Single-tap** – this is the one you'll use most and it opens apps, selects items in lists, opens text boxes, follows online links, activates options and enters text on the keyboard

- **Double-tap** – in web pages a double-tap zooms in – double-tapping again zooms back out. This also works with pictures

- **Two-finger tap** – when in a maps app, this gesture zooms out

- **Swipe** – dragging a finger across the screen, or up and down, in a swiping motion enables you to scroll across and down the screen, scroll through lists, and drag items to different positions

- **Flick** – a quick flick on the screen will scroll faster than a swipe. The faster the flick, the faster the movement

- **Spread and pinch** – touching the screen with two fingers and spreading them apart will zoom in on a screen, while pinching them together will zoom out

- **Press and hold** – this gesture is used in apps where text can be selected, such as a web page or email. Press and hold on a word and you will bring up editing options such as Copy, Select All, etc. You can also get dictionary definitions in this way

- **Tap at the top of the screen** – tapping once at the top of the screen will quickly take you to the top of a web page, list or email message

- **Four-finger swipe** – swiping upwards with four fingers opens the multitasking interface

- **Press and drag** – press on any clear part of the screen and drag downwards to open your iPad's Spotlight search feature

The Multitasking Interface

The multitasking capabilities built-in to the iPad allow you to do a number of things. These are:

View Open Apps & Switch Between Them Quickly

In a situation where you are working with two or more apps simultaneously, it can be very useful to be able to instantly switch from one to the other. Because the apps aren't closed when doing this, their current states, including data, are saved in the iPad's memory. Alternatively, you may just want to see what apps are currently open.

In either case, you need to activate the App Switcher. This is done by double-pressing the Home button (or using the four-finger swipe).

A screen will now open showing stacked images of all the apps currently open on the iPad – you may need to flick right and left to see them all. This is demonstrated in the image above. To switch to a particular app, just tap on its image and it will open.

Close Apps

As a general rule, it is not necessary to close apps as they use very little in the way of system resources. Should you wish to do so for some reason however, activate the App Switcher to reveal all the open apps. Each app can be closed by swiping its image upwards. It will disappear from view to be replaced by the next open app.

Slide Over

Slide Over lets you interact with a second app without having to leave the app that you are currently using. This is a very useful feature that, for example, lets you quickly check your text messages, emails, access the Internet, make notes, all the while keeping your main app in view.

To use Slide Over, place your finger at the right of the screen and swipe across to the left. A vertical list of all the apps on the iPad appears – scroll down and tap the one you require. The selected app will open in a panel at the right, and the main app will be darkened to indicate it has been temporarily disabled. When you want to switch back to it, just tap on the screen.

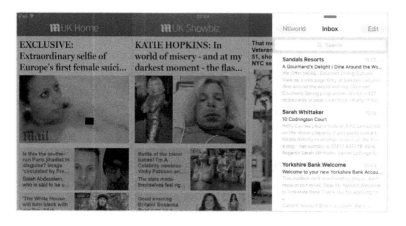

In the example above, the main app on the left is the Safari web browser and the secondary app on the right is the Mail app.

To return to the vertical app list and open a different app, swipe downwards from the top of the panel. To close the panel, just tap anywhere on the part of the screen occupied by the main app – this will also re-enable the app.

Split View

Split View is similar in concept to the Slide Over feature but is more capable. Instead of just being able to use one of the open apps as with Slide Over, it lets you keep both of them, not just visible, but also active.

Activating Split View is done by sliding your finger in from the right-edge of the screen, in the same manner as for Slide Over. When the slide over panel is visible, tap on the small white handle. The app on the left will then shift over, adjusting in size so that all controls are visible and active. You will notice that the white handle is still present and can be used to adjust the amount of screen each app takes up. Drag the handle to the left and release it in the middle of the screen to give each app the same amount of space.

Sliding the app divider further to the left will result in the first app being closed, and the second app taking over the entire screen. Note that the Split View feature is only available in the Pro, Air 2, and Mini 4 iPad models.

Picture-in-Picture (PIP)

Picture-in-picture is a new feature that lets you watch a video while working in another app. The video will play in a small window in a corner of the screen and can be dragged to any corner. It can also be dragged off the screen to reveal more of the display. A sliver of the video will remain in view, however, allowing it to be dragged back into full view whenever you want.

PIP can be activated in two ways. The first is to start playing the video with the Videos app and then tap the PIP button on the toolbar at the bottom (if you don't see the toolbar, tap once on the screen to bring it up). The second is to press the Home button while a video is playing – wherever you go in the iPad from then on, the video will follow you around and be visible in the lower right-hand corner.

You can resize the video window with pinching or stretching gestures. By tapping on the video, you'll reveal three controls – these let you deactivate PIP, play or pause the clip, or close it completely.

Picture-in-Picture works on all the iPad models. However, applications using proprietary video players do not support PIP – this includes popular video playing apps such as YouTube and Netflix.

The Control Center

The iPad's Control Center is a quickly accessible panel that provides access to a number of frequently used controls.

To open it, place your finger on the bottom edge of the screen and swipe upwards – the panel will slide into view. By default, it can be opened from the Lock screen, the Home screen, and from within open apps.

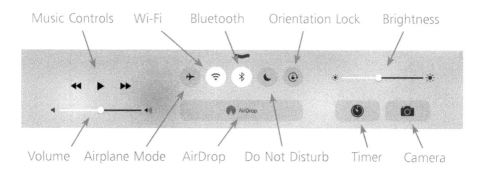

Music Controls   Wi-Fi   Bluetooth   Orientation Lock   Brightness

Volume   Airplane Mode   AirDrop   Do Not Disturb   Timer   Camera

Available controls include AirDrop file-sharing settings, screen brightness, the Camera app, the timer, system volume, and music playback. You can also enable and disable Airplane mode, Wi-Fi, Bluetooth, Do Not Disturb, Screen Orientation Lock, and system mute in the Control Center.

Some of these are self-explanatory. Others that may not be, however, are:

AirDrop – AirDrop is a method of transferring data wirelessly from one iOS device to another. It allows users to easily share pictures, video and other supported data with anyone nearby who is using a supported iOS device or Mac computer.

There are no restrictions on the size of the documents that AirDrop will transfer. AirDrop devices need to be within 10 meters of each other for the system to work. Currently, few applications support this feature.

Bluetooth – Bluetooth is a wireless network technology that creates short-range connections between suitably equipped devices at distances up to about 10 meters. A typical use is listening to music on your iPad with a set of Bluetooth wireless headphones. Note that on the iPad, Bluetooth is also required for the AirDrop feature to work.

Wi-Fi – Wi-Fi is another wireless technology that allows electronic devices to exchange data, or connect to the Internet, without the need for a physical connection. The vast majority of current computing devices, including personal computers, video-game consoles, smartphones, digital cameras, tablets, and digital audio players are equipped with Wi-Fi technology.

Wi-Fi enables these devices to connect to a network resource such as the Internet, via a wireless network access point known as a hotspot. Typically, it has a range of about 150 feet indoors and about 300 feet outdoors.

Hotspot coverage can comprise an area as small as a single room (walls block Wi-Fi signals) or many square miles (achieved by using multiple overlapping access points).

Orientation Lock – we mentioned on page 19 that the iPad can be held in either Landscape or Portrait mode. By default, each time you swivel the device it will change from one to the other. If you would rather keep it in one particular mode, you can use this control to set it quickly.

Airplane Mode – Airplane mode disables the wireless features of your iPad in order to comply with airline regulations. When it is activated, the following wireless connections and services are turned off:

- Cellular (voice and data)

- Wi-Fi

- Bluetooth

- Global Positioning Systems (GPS)

- Location services

Note that if allowed by the aircraft operator, and applicable laws and regulations, you can enable Wi-Fi and Bluetooth while in Airplane mode.

Do Not Disturb – the Do Not Disturb control lets you silence calls, alerts, and notifications. If you open the Settings app and tap 'Do Not Disturb', you'll see various configuration options for this control. These include:

- Automatic scheduling that lets you set a specific period for which the feature will be active

- Accepting calls from certain people while the feature is on. Options are: Everyone, No One, or All Contacts

- Accepting a second FaceTime call from the same person within three minutes of the first. So if someone needs to talk to you urgently, a second call within three minutes will be accepted

- You can set Do Not Disturb to be always active or only active when the iPad is locked

The Lock Screen

When you switch on your iPad, or the device is inactive for five minutes, it defaults to a Lock screen. This is a power-saving feature designed to save the battery, and is roughly equivalent to the Sleep option on computers. To get into the iPad, slide the button at the bottom.

You can change the default settings for the Lock screen by opening the Settings app and going to General > Auto-Lock.

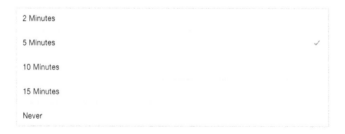

Here, you will be able to specify the time before auto-lock kicks in – 2, 5, 10, or 15 minutes. You can also choose Never, which disables the Lock screen completely.

Note that you can activate the Lock screen manually at any time by clicking the on/off button once. Also, do not be mislead by the name 'Lock screen' – it does not prevent unauthorized access to your iPad. For this you need to use Touch ID or a passcode as we see in Chapter 11.

Notifications & Notification Center

Notifications

Notifications is an iOS feature that enables apps to notify you of new messages or events without you having to actually open the app – email messages being a typical example. When a notification is generated, it will be presented on the Lock screen and also in the Notification Center.

Notifications come in four types:

- **Sound** – a sound effect that indicates an event has occurred

- **Alert** – a message that pops up on the screen. This has to be dismissed with a tap before you can resume what you were doing

- **Banner** – a message that appears at the top of the screen and disappears automatically after a few seconds

- **Badge** – a red icon at the top-right corner of an app icon. It displays a number that can indicate various things. For example, the number of unread emails in the Mail app

Notification Center

The iPad's Notification Center is designed to help you make the most of the Notifications feature. It collects all the alerts and banners as they come in and displays them in one easily accessible location.

To open the Notification Center, just swipe down from the top edge of the screen. On the left-hand side it will show you the Today view, which displays the date, events from the Calendar app, Reminder items, and a summary of the schedule for the following day.

At the top right-hand side are two options – Widgets and Notifications. Tap the former and you will see information from any apps on your iPad that have a widget function. Widgets are tiny applications that carry out a specific action and are often part of a larger application. Typical examples of widgets are weather apps and calculators.

Most widgets provide basic information in the Notification Center, such as news headlines and sports results. If you want to read the full story, tap the widget to open it's parent app in full screen view.

If you want widgets other than the default ones provided with your iPad, you have to go to the App Store to get them. Note that you can't actually get widgets as such – you have to download an app that offers a widget function.

A good example is the Kindle app. This offers a widget that shows the books you are currently reading, and provides a link that allows you to open them on the iPad at the current page.

The second option is Notifications. This shows notifications from other apps as we see in the image below:

28

The type of apps that typically show notifications are email apps and social media apps such as Facebook and Twitter. As soon as you install them, they will begin posting notifications. Other apps wait until you give them permission.

To configure which apps will and won't show notifications, open the Settings app and tap Notifications (the 4th setting from the top). In the Notification Style section, you will see a list of all the apps on your iPad capable of showing notifications. Tap on one and you will see the following:

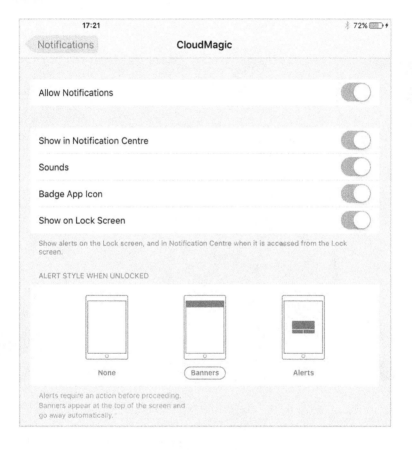

To set the app to allow notifications, toggle the 'Allow Notifications' setting to On. The 'Show in Notification Center' setting determines whether or not the app shows notifications in the Notification Center. You will also see various other settings which vary from app to app, such as 'Show on Lock screen'.

In the 'Alert Style When Unlocked' section, you will see three options that determine how the notifications appear visually when the iPad is unlocked. You can choose None, Banners (the alert appears at the top of whichever screen you are in), or Alerts (the alert appears in a pop-up window).

Spotlight Search

One of the best things about computers in general is that the search facilities provided with these devices make it so easy to locate things.

Your iPad's Spotlight Search facility is no exception and, with it, you can find literally everything that is on the device. Whether you are looking for someone's contact information, a movie, a song, an event, or a book, just type in the name and everything with that word in it will appear in the search results.

To open Spotlight Search, place your finger on an empty part of the Home screen and flick downwards.

Enter your search term in the box at the top and a list of results will automatically appear – you may need to scroll down to see them all (if the keyboard is in the way, tap the Keyboard options key at the bottom-right of the keyboard to hide it – see page 34). You will also see options for searching Wikipedia, the iTunes Store, and Microsoft's Bing search engine.

Tap an item in the list to open it. Note that Spotlight Search can also be used to find and open apps.

Configuration options can be found in the Settings app. Tap General on the left and then tap Spotlight Search on the right. Here, you can choose which apps and related content are searched.

Siri

Siri is a built-in, voice-controlled personal assistant for the iPad. It provides you with a way of interacting with your device that doesn't involve having to tap away at the touchscreen or typing on the keyboard. Instead, you speak to Siri and Siri speaks back to you.

What Can Siri Do?
You can ask Siri questions and it will come up with an answer, or issue commands for it to execute on your behalf.

Siri can send messages and emails you speak into the microphone and it can read incoming messages out to you when they arrive. It can give you directions. It can listen to your questions and search not just your iPad for the answer but also the Internet.

It can set alarms and reminders, not to mention calendar events. Siri will play your music and video, and let you dictate text into documents or, indeed, any text input field.

Activating Siri
The default way to start Siri is to press and hold the Home button (if you are using a headset with a microphone button, press and hold the button). You will then see a message that says 'What can I help you with?'

Wait for the next screen and you'll see a microphone at the bottom. Tap the microphone and then speak your question or command – Siri will attempt to do your bidding.

However, there is another way to activate Siri. Open the Settings app and go to General > Siri. Toggle the on/off button next to 'Allow Hey, Siri' to the On position. Now you can activate Siri from any screen by simply saying 'Hey Siri'.

There is a proviso here though – the iPad must be connected to a power source; if it is not, Hey Siri will not work. The reason for this is that the feature requires the device to be constantly listening for your voice commands, which means it would be constantly drawing power from the battery. Limiting 'Hey, Siri…' to when the iPad is receiving power means the battery won't be affected.

While in Siri's settings, you can disable the feature if you want to, set the language Siri uses, and set the gender.

You can also specify your personal details so Siri knows who you are, what your telephone numbers are, and where you are located. This lets you say things like 'Call home' or 'Give me directions to work'. Do it by tapping My Info and selecting your own contact from the All Contacts list.

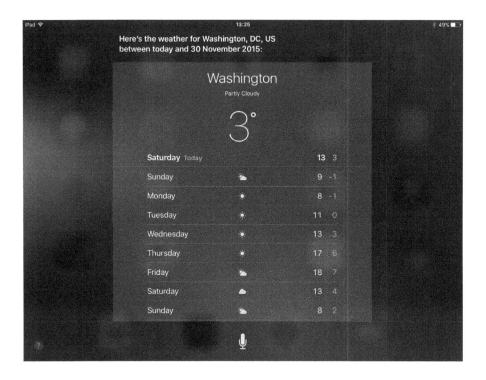

Above, we see Siri's response to the question 'what is the weather in washington?'

CHAPTER 3

The Keyboard

Your iPad does not come with a physical keyboard – this is one of the reasons the device is so small and portable. Instead, it is equipped with what's known as a 'virtual keyboard'.

In this chapter, we will see exactly how this virtual keyboard works and how you can set it up to suit your method of working. We explain how to enter and edit text, plus show you some very useful keyboard shortcuts that will save a lot of time and effort.

We also take a look at some third-party keyboards and see how they can be used instead of the default iPad keyboard.

The Virtual Keyboard

As we mentioned in the introduction to this chapter, the iPad does not provide a physical keyboard. Instead, in an effort to make the device as compact and light as possible, it uses an electronic, or virtual, version.

You won't actually see the keyboard until you open an app that requires text to be entered. Just tap in the text area provided by the app and the keyboard will slide up from the bottom of the screen. For example, a web page search box or an email message window.

For those of you not familiar with keyboards, it may be helpful to highlight certain of the keys at this point.

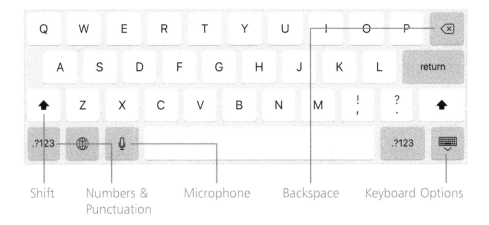

Shift   Numbers &   Microphone   Backspace   Keyboard Options
          Punctuation

Shift key – press this key to shift between upper-case and lower-case. When you have typed the upper-case character, the keyboard automatically reverts to lower-case. Double-tap the key for Caps Lock.

Numbers & Punctuation key – this key switches from letters, to numbers and punctuation marks. When in the latter mode, the Shift key turns into the Symbols key.

cont'd

Tap the Symbols key to access they Symbols keyboard as shown below:

Microphone – if you want to use the iPad's dictation feature, then pressing this key will activate it.

Backspace key – pressing this key deletes characters to the left of the cursor. Three modes are available:

1. Press once to delete a single character

2. Press and hold down to delete continuously

3. Press and hold down for four seconds. After four seconds entire words are deleted

Return key – this key moves the cursor to the next line.

Keyboard Options – you will find that the keyboard sometimes gets in the way of what you are doing – tapping this key removes it from the screen.

Note that the iPad's keyboard is contextual – it presents keys that are related to the task in hand. For example, you will see different keys when typing an email than when typing a text message.

It is also possible to use a full-size physical keyboard with the iPad. This is useful if you have to do an extensive amount of typing. An example is the Apple wireless keyboard (shown below), which connects to the iPad via Bluetooth. We look at some others on page 50.

Manipulating the Keyboard

When opened, the keyboard's default position is at the bottom of the screen; for most purposes this is the logical place for it to be. However, this may not always be the case and, if so, it can be moved to somewhere more suitable.

Undocking the Keyboard
To move the keyboard, it must first be undocked from the bottom of the screen. Do this as follows:

1. Press and hold the Keyboard Options key at the bottom-right corner of the keyboard

2. You will see a menu offering two options: Undock and Split – select the Undock option

3. The keyboard will now be released from the bottom and moved to the middle of the screen

4. With the keyboard undocked, if you press the Keyboard Options button and drag at the same time, you will be able to move the keyboard to different positions on the screen. Note that you have to start dragging before the Undock/Split menu appears otherwise it won't move – this can be a bit fiddly!

cont'd

Splitting the Keyboard

It is also possible to split the keyboard into separate halves and place them on either side of the screen. Many people find it is easier to use this way, particularly those who type with their thumbs.

To do it:

1. Press and hold the Keyboard Options key at the bottom-right corner of the keyboard

2. In the Options menu, select Split

3. The keyboard is split and each half is placed on opposite sides at the middle of the screen as we see below:

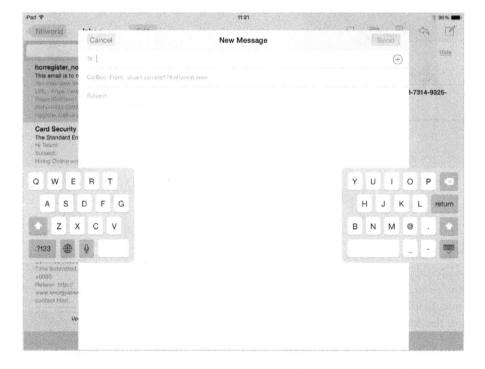

4. If you want to move the split keyboard up or down, you can do so by pressing the Keyboard Options button and dragging it to the required position as we explained in Step 4 on the previous page

5. To return the keyboard to its default position at the bottom of the screen, press the Keyboard Options button again and select Dock and Merge

Entering Text

To enter text in an app, open it and tap once in a text field – this action will open the keyboard. All you have to do now is type in your text. As you do so, you may notice two things:

Auto-Correction
Auto-correct is a feature that attempts to prevent you making spelling mistakes. If it thinks that you are misspelling a word, it will open a little pop-up window below the word suggesting what it considers to be the correct spelling.

The feature can also be used as a shortcut that enables you to complete a word with a single tap. The problem with Auto-correct is that it often jumps in too soon and offers a wrong word. If you then tap Return or type a space or punctuation mark, it will assume you want to use its suggested word and type it on the screen.

However, you can prevent it doing this by simply tapping anywhere in the pop-up window. Alternatively, you can disable the feature in the keyboard's settings as we explain on page 43.

Check Spelling
If you do make a spelling mistake, it will be underlined in red (this can also be disabled in the keyboard's settings).

When you have finished typing, just tap the Keyboard Options key to remove the keyboard from the screen.

Editing Text

Editing text on a tablet is never going to be as quick as on a computer or laptop. Both the screen and keyboard are much smaller, plus touchscreen control is not as precise as it is with a mouse or touchpad. Nevertheless, it's surprising just what is possible with the iPad.

Positioning the cursor

Getting the cursor precisely where you want it is an essential part of text editing. One way of doing it is to use the Backspace key to backtrack, which of course deletes everything as it goes along. Fairly obviously, this is a far from ideal way of doing it.

A much better method is to tap and hold on the text to be edited. You will then see the text beneath your finger, and the cursor, enlarged inside a magnifying glass. By dragging your finger left and right, you will be able to easily position the cursor exactly where you want it.

Selecting and Copying/Moving Text

Your options here depend on whether the text is editable or non-editable. A web page is a good example of the latter and the only option you will have is to copy.

To do this, tap and hold the required word. You will then see the word has been highlighted between two blue selection handles. Above this will be a menu offering various options that include Copy. Tap Copy and then open the app into which you are going to paste the word. Tap once in the text field and a menu will open offering a Paste option. Tap Paste and the word will be pasted into the text field.

Using this method, you can copy and paste single words, whole blocks of text or even an entire page. All you have to do is adjust the selection handles by dragging them up and down, and left and right. Once you have made your selection, click Copy and paste it where you want it to go. Below we see a selected sentence:

In the case of editable text, such as text you've created in a note, email, text message or word processor, the procedure is much the same.

Tap and hold anywhere in the text. When you see the magnifying glass, remove your finger and you will see the toolbar as before. This time, it will be showing some different options as we see below:

- **Select** – choose this option if you want to select just some of the text. You will then see the selection handles while the toolbar above will now offer even more options – Cut, Copy Paste, Replace..., B*I*U, Define, Speak..., Share and Indent

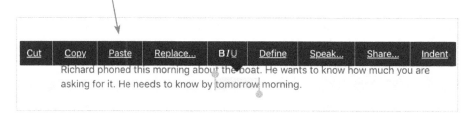

  Choose Cut to remove the text, Copy to copy it, Paste to replace it with text you have copied from elsewhere, Replace... to replace it with a suggestion and, if it's a word, Define to see the definition of the word from the built-in dictionary

- **Select All** – tapping Select All will return the same options as above with the exception of Replace

- **Paste** – if you have previously copied some text, clicking Paste will replace the text ('tomorrow' in the example above) with the copied text

Note that you get different options depending on the app in use – the Mail app is a good example of this. In addition to Cut, Copy and Paste, you will also see options that allow you to insert pictures and video, plus add attachments.

As already mentioned, you will notice that as you type, any misspelled words are underlined in red. If you tap on the word, you will see some suggestions as to the correct spelling. If the one you want is there, just tap it and it will replace the misspelled word.

The Trackpad

Still on the subject of selecting and moving text, iOS 9 introduces a new method of doing so. This is the Trackpad feature which, when activated, emulates the type of trackpad commonly seen on laptops and Personal Digital Assistants (PDAs). It allows you to control the cursor by sliding a finger around the keyboard.

To activate the trackpad, place two fingers on the keyboard as shown below:

Immediately, the keys fade away to provide a trackpad-like surface for cursor manipulation. Move your fingers and the cursor moves with you.

To select a section of text with the trackpad, position the cursor anywhere in the text and then tap the screen with two fingers – the selection handles duly appear. You can now select the required text with just one finger.

Having done so, tap anywhere in the selected text to bring up a toolbar of editing options – as already explained, these will differ from app to app.

Predictive Text

Your iPad's keyboard has quite a few tricks up its sleeve, one of which is the ability to 'predict' what you are intending to type – this is Predictive Text.

The Predictive Text feature notes the text that you enter over time and uses it to build a customized, local dictionary of words and phrases that you commonly use. It then 'scores' those words by the probability of you using them again. Essentially, it learns as it goes along and becomes progressively more accurate.

By default, the feature is turned off – enable it in the keyboard's settings (see pages 43-44) or as described at the bottom of this page. When Predictive Text is activated, you will see a QuickType bar at the top of the keyboard. Initially, the bar will show I, The and I'm. If you want to start a sentence with any of these just tap on it.

As you type more text, the feature offers suggestions. These can often save you from having to type out a long word in full – just tap to use it.

A quick way of enabling/disabling Predictive Text is by pressing and holding the Globe icon at the bottom-left of the keyboard. A menu will open showing the relevant option.

Keyboard Settings

As with many of the iPad's functions, there are a number of settings available for the keyboard. These let you customize it to suit your way of working.

You can access these settings by:

1. Tapping the Settings app on the Home screen

2. Tapping the General tab

3. Scrolling down to and tapping Keyboard

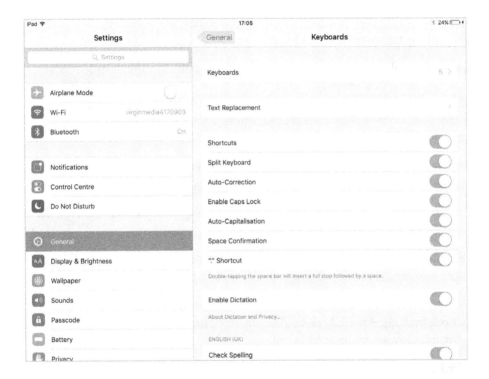

The available settings are shown on the right of the window and include:

Keyboards – you are not restricted to the default iPad keyboard – this setting lets you use other keyboards as we explain on page 49.

Text Replacement – a very useful keyboard feature, this lets you associate a phrase or sentence with a single keyboard character. We explain how to set this up on page 46.

Auto-Correction – this feature attempts to correct you when it thinks you have made a typing mistake.

Enable Caps Lock – initially, you may think the iPad's keyboard does not provide a Caps lock function. However, it does and the way to activate it is by double-tapping the Shift key.

When you do it will turn from:

this   to this

Don't forget though, you need to enable the feature in the keyboard's settings by tapping the switch to the On position.

Auto-Capitalization – auto-capitalization automatically capitalizes letters at the beginning of a sentence. When enabled, every time you type a character that indicates the end of a sentence, i.e. a period, question mark or exclamation mark, and follow it with a space, the feature assumes you want to end the sentence and begin a new one.

Accordingly, it automatically activates the Shift key so that the next word is capitalized.

"." Shortcut – when this is enabled, double-tapping the space bar inserts a full stop followed by a space.

Enable Dictation – the iPad's Dictation feature lets you speak to the iPad and have your words converted into text. We explain how to use this feature on page 48.

Check Spelling – the Check Spelling feature checks your spelling as you type. Any mistakes are underlined in red.

Predictive – this lets the keyboard suggest related words as we explained on page 42.

Fuzzy Pinyin – Pinyin allows users to input Chinese characters by entering the pinyin of a character and then presenting them with a list of possible characters with that pronunciation. Fuzzy pinyin makes allowances for regional accents that would otherwise make it difficult to distinguish between similar sounding syllables of pinyin.

Keyboard Tricks & Shortcuts

There are a number of tricks and shortcuts that can be used with the iPad's keyboard. For people who do serious amounts of typing, these can be extremely useful:

Quickly insert numbers & punctuation – to insert numbers and punctuation, you tap the .?123 key, tap the required character and then tap the ABC key to revert to the letters keyboard.

A quicker way is to tap the .?123 key but instead of releasing it and going to the required character, keep your finger on the screen and slide it to the key you want. When it has been selected, release the key and the keyboard will automatically revert to letters.

More quick punctuation – swiping up on the Comma key will insert an apostrophe; swiping up on the Period key inserts a quotation mark.

Quick capital letters – rather than engage the Shift key every time you need to type a capital letter, just press and hold the Shift key and drag your finger to the letter you want to capitalize.

Related characters – pressing and holding a character will, in many cases, open a list of related characters above the key. For example, other currencies from the currency key and accented versions of letter keys.

Emoticons – if you want to insert emoticons in your emails and text messages, tap the Globe key at the bottom-left of the keyboard next to the .?123 key. You will see a categorized list of hundreds of icons and emoticons as shown on the image at the top of the next page.

Tap the category icons at the bottom to browse through the lists of emoticons.

Quick spacing – tap the space bar with three fingers to get three spaces, with four fingers to get four spaces and with five fingers to get five spaces.

Website extensions – when you are typing a website address in an Internet browser, instead of typing the extension, press and hold the Period key. A menu will open showing a list of common extensions such as .com, .co.uk – just select the one you want.

Text Replacement – if you type a certain phrase or sentence often, you can set a shortcut for it which, when typed, automatically expands to the full phrase.

To set this up:

1. Open the Settings app and go to General > Keyboard

2. Tap Text Replacement

3. Tap the + icon at the top-right of the window

4. Type your phrase into the Phrase box

5. Type the shortcut you want to associate with the phrase in the Shortcut box. Then tap Save

Shortcut Bar

We mentioned Predictive Text and the QuickType bar on page 42. A new shortcuts feature in iOS 9 makes use of the free space on either side of the central Predictive Text section. These shortcuts provide fast and easy access to common editing commands. When using the Mail app for example, they include undo, redo, and paste to the left side, and bold, italic, underline, and attach pictures and attachments to the right.

Undo, Redo, Paste   BIU, Attachments

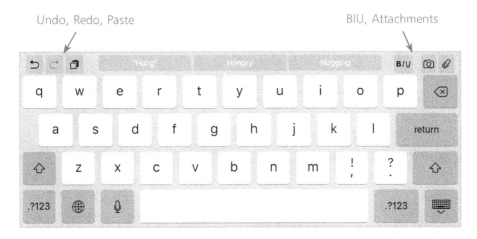

The shortcuts offered can change depending on context, and vary between apps. For example, in Mail, if text has been selected the undo and redo shortcuts change to cut and copy as we see below:

As another example, when using the Notes app you will get shortcuts that let you format titles, headings, and bulleted and numbered lists, plus add pictures and drawing tools.

Dictation

For users who find it difficult to use keyboards, and for those occasions when a serious amount of typing is required, the iPad provides a very useful feature called Dictation. We saw on pages 43-44 how to enable it in the iPad's settings.

You can use Dictation anywhere you can enter text. For example, you can dictate emails, text messages, reminders, notes, and even search terms in Safari's search box. Whenever you see the microphone icon next to the Space bar on the keyboard, the Dictation feature is available to you.

Just tap in a text field, tap the microphone icon and then start talking. When you're finished, tap Done and then wait for your words to be processed. It can take a few seconds for text to appear.

Dictation Tips

Generally, the Dictation feature works well. However, observing the tips below can improve things considerably:

- Talk directly into the microphone

- Try dictating with a headset that has an integral microphone; this is particularly effective in a noisy environment

- Make sure you are connected to the Internet via Wi-Fi. Dictation requires that your voice be sent to a server where it is recognized and transcribed and then sent back to your iPad. The process works better when you're using a Wi-Fi network

- Speak punctuation and symbols. To include punctuation in your dictation, you need to say 'comma,' 'period,' 'hyphen,' and so on. Watch out for language differences. For instance, if you're using UK English, you need to say 'full stop' instead of 'period'

- Be careful with acronyms – you can use some but not all. Experiment to see which work and which don't. When spelling acronyms, make sure you pause between letters just long enough for them to be discrete

Third-Party Keyboards

You are not restricted to the keyboard provided with your iPad. There is actually a huge number of keyboard apps available from the App Store – many of these provide features and options that the default keyboard doesn't.

There is also the option of using a physical keyboard that connects to the iPad via Bluetooth – we look at this on the next page.

To see what's available with regard to virtual keyboards, tap the App Store icon on the Home screen and then enter 'keyboard' in the search box at the top-right. Find a keyboard and download it to your iPad (we explain how to download and install apps on pages 71-72).

Setting Up a Virtual Keyboard
Having downloaded and installed a keyboard, it now needs to be configured. The procedure for this is:

1. Open the Settings app

2. Tap General

3. Tap Keyboard

4. Tap Keyboards at the top of the screen

5. Tap 'Add New Keyboard...'

6. Under 'Third-Party keyboards', tap the keyboard you've just installed

7. The keyboard is now added to the keyboard list

That done, now open the default keyboard and go to the Globe key at the left of the space bar. Press and hold this key and a pop-up window will open showing your keyboard list. Keeping your finger on the screen, slide it to the new keyboard and then let go.

The default keyboard will now be replaced by the new keyboard. An example is shown below:

Physical Keyboards

Virtual keyboards are all well and good and certainly have their place, but for sheer ease of use nothing beats a proper physical keyboard. The latter are also far more suitable for older people who tend to find virtual keyboards fiddly.

We've already mentioned the Apple wireless keyboard and on this page we'll look at some other types of physical keyboard that can be used with the iPad. These all communicate with the device via a Bluetooth connection that needs to be set up as we explain at the bottom of the page. First though, we'll take a look at what's available:

- **Folio-Case Keyboards** – the most common type, these keyboards are integrated into a full-body, folio-style case that also protects the iPad. The all-in-one design of folio keyboards is convenient, and most make it easy to type on your lap – a desk or table is not required

- **Clamshell Keyboards** – these effectively turn an iPad into a small laptop with the iPad as the laptop screen, and the keyboard as the laptop's base. Key quality is usually better than with folio-case keyboards, the laptop style design works well for typing on your lap, and most offer a good range of screen angles

- **Keyboard Shells** – these are the thinnest and lightest of the keyboards. They integrate a thin keyboard into a rigid shell that protects the iPad's screen. When you're ready to type, pop the iPad out of the shell, position it in a prop-up slot above the keyboard and start typing

Setting Up a Physical Keyboard

As we mentioned at the top of the page, physical keyboards are Bluetooth devices and need to be set up. The procedure for doing this is:

1. Switch the keyboard on

2. On the iPad, open the Settings app and then tap Bluetooth at the right of the screen

3. After a few moments, you'll see your Bluetooth keyboard appear in the Devices list. Tap on it to activate the connection. When you see the word 'Connected' next to it, the keyboard is ready for operation

CHAPTER 4

Setting Up Your iPad

When you first switch on your iPad, you will be presented with a setup wizard that walks you through a series of configuration settings. We explain what these settings are so that you select the right options.

There are also a number of other settings that you will need to configure in order to set up the iPad to suit your own way of working, needs and personality.

Setup Wizard

When an iPad is run for the first time, it offers a setup wizard designed to help the user get off to a flying start. Whether or not you follow the wizard is entirely up to you – if you wish, you can skip it and configure the device as you go along.

However, as the wizard does deal with some important aspects of the iPad, such as setting up an Apple ID (needed to use the Apps and iTunes Stores), setting up a Wi-Fi connection, iCloud, and Touch ID amongst other things, our recommendation is that you follow the wizard's prompts.

Most, if not all, of them will probably have to be done at some point anyway so it may as well be right at the start.

1. First, you will be prompted to select your country or region

2. Next, you will be asked to specify a Wi-Fi network in order to begin device activation. Wi-Fi is a technology that allows you to wirelessly connect to a local-area network, and will allow you to browse the Internet, connect to the App and iTunes Stores, send and receive email, and use many other features of your iPad

3. Once you are connected, you will be asked whether you wish to enable Location Services. This is an iPad feature that allows location-aware apps, such as Maps and the Safari web browser, to use information from cellular, Wi-Fi, and Global Positioning Systems (GPS) networks to determine your location

    A typical example of how location services is used is Yellow Pages apps that use your location to help you find nearby coffee shops, theaters, ATM's, etc. Many of the apps available for the iPad rely on the Location Services feature, so we recommend you enable it when prompted

4. At the next stage, you will be asked whether you want to set up your iPad as a new device, or restore its content and settings from a backup. You would choose the latter option if you have an older iPad and want to transfer its contents and settings to the new iPad

5. You are going to need an Apple ID, or account. If you already have one, you can associate it with the iPad now by signing in. If you don't have an ID, you are prompted to create one.

    Note that your Apple ID can be used with any other Apple devices you may have, or later acquire. It enables you to use any Apple service, such as the iTunes and App Stores, iCloud, iMessage, FaceTime, Game Center, and iBooks

Creating an Apple ID is very simple; all that's required is your name, date of birth, email address, a password, and a security question and answer

6. Agree to Apple's terms and conditions

7. Next, you are asked whether you wish to use iCloud. This is a service from Apple that gives you free online storage space that you can use to keep your devices synchronized.

   Synchronization is the transfer of data, such as music, pictures and documents, between your Apple devices. iCloud does it behind the scenes for you automatically

   iCloud can also automatically backup your iPad and restore that backup should it ever be necessary to do so. Plus, of course, it can be used for data storage purposes

   So if you envisage ever needing to transfer data between your iPad and another Apple device, create a backup, or simply store stuff online, setting up an iCloud account is a must. We look at the subject of iCloud and other related services in more detail in Chapter 12

8. Owners of Pro, Air 2, and Mini 4 iPads are now offered the option to set up Apple's fingerprint recognition feature, Touch ID. This allows you to use your finger rather than having to enter passwords and passcodes

9. If you choose not to set up Touch ID, you will be asked whether you wish to set up a passcode to secure your iPad. Just enter a four- or six-digit digit code when prompted and, henceforth, you'll have to enter the code to unlock the iPad. It's not essential that you do this but it is recommended

10. Set up iCloud Keychain. This feature keeps your website user names and passwords, credit card information, and Wi-Fi network information up-to-date across all of your Apple devices

11. Enter your phone number. This will be used to verify your identity when using your iCloud security code

12. Approve or disapprove Siri. As we have already seen, Siri is a voice recognition feature that lets you speak to your iPad to issue commands, or request information

13. Finally, you are asked whether you are willing to send information back to Apple for diagnostic purposes. Doing this will help Apple to improve the device both for you and other users, so we recommend that you do

Settings App

On page 24, we explained how the Control Center can be used to adjust frequently used settings such as screen brightness and volume, and access functions such as the camera.

However, there are literally hundreds of other settings with which you can set up your iPad to suit your needs. Many of these are one-off settings that, once done, won't need to be touched again, or very rarely. They can all be accessed through the Settings app.

The app opens in the following view:

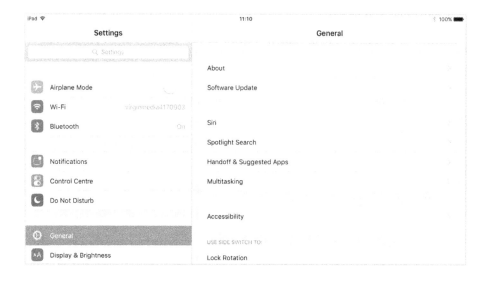

At the left, you will see headings for the various types of settings and, on the right, a list of settings for the type selected. You will notice that the headings are grouped by type.

The top three headings – Airplane Mode, Wi-Fi and Bluetooth – are all network related. Below these are settings for Notifications, Control Center and Do Not Disturb – these determine how you interact with your iPad.

Moving down the list of headings, the final group includes all the apps installed on the iPad. Tapping one will reveal any settings available for the app. Some will have more than others, and some will offer none at all.

A new feature in the Settings app is the search box at the top-left. This has been added due to the ever increasing number of iPad settings and lets you quickly find settings that would otherwise involve tapping through a number of screens. As you type in the searchbox, results appear below.

Name Your iPad

Your iPad needs a name, which is why the setup wizard asks you to specify one. You may think it's so you can put your personal stamp on the device but actually it's more to do with backing up and recovery purposes.

Every backup you make is identifiable by the iPad's name and the date it was created. If you sync your data across several devices, by giving each device a unique name, you are able to differentiate between multiple backups.

You can change the name to something more suitable or cool sounding at any time.

The way to do it is:

1. Open the Settings app

2. On the left, tap General to open the General settings screen

3. Right at the top, tap About to open the About screen

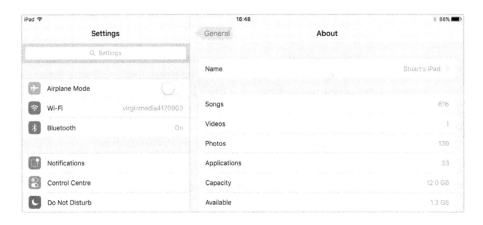

4. Tap Name at the top – you will see a Name box displaying the current name. Tap the box to open the Edit screen and then enter the desired name

Below the Name setting, you'll see some general information about your iPad. Much of this is statistical, such as the number of songs, videos, photos and apps on the device.

Perhaps more useful is the amount of available storage capacity – those of you who use the iPad for storing media will definitely need to keep an eye on this.

Screen Brightness

The level of brightness on your iPad is an important issue in more ways than one. First, it needs to be at a level that's easy on the eye. Second, reducing the brightness reduces the device's power consumption and thus extends battery life. There are two ways to adjust it:

The first, and the quickest, is to open the Control Center by swiping up from the bottom edge of the screen – you'll see the Brightness control at the top-right. Adjust it by dragging the slider left or right.

The second is to go to the Settings app > Display & Brightness. At the top, you'll see the Brightness control slider. Below is an auto-brightness option, which is enabled by default.

Auto-brightness employs a built-in light sensor to measure the ambient light level of your surroundings. It then uses this as a reference point on which to base the automatic adjustment of the iPad's brightness. Because the process is automatic, the brightness of the screen should always be suitable for the current reading conditions. The control dims the screen when you are in dark conditions and brightens it when you have more light around you.

Generally, the Auto-Brightness feature does a good job of handling your iPad's brightness levels and most users will be well served by it.

Below the Brightness control, you will see options for setting the size of the text displayed on the iPad, and making all the text bold. These may be of interest to the older generation whose eyesight is perhaps not quite as good as it used to be.

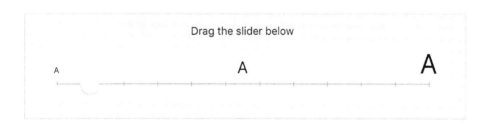

Wallpaper

Many people are happy to use the default iPad wallpaper. Others, however, either because they simply don't like it, or because they want to personalize their device, will want to change it.

This can be done in two ways:

The first is to open the Settings app and tap Wallpaper on the left of the screen. You'll now see your current wallpaper and how it looks on both the Lock screen and the Home screen.

Tap 'Choose a New Wallpaper' to open a screen that offers a choice of two different types of wallpaper – Dynamic (these contain moving objects within the wallpaper) and Stills. Tap the required type to bring up a list of available wallpapers.

Below we see the Stills collection. Tap one and the image will open in a full-screen preview. At the bottom, you'll see options to Cancel or set it as Lock Screen, Home Screen, and Set Both.

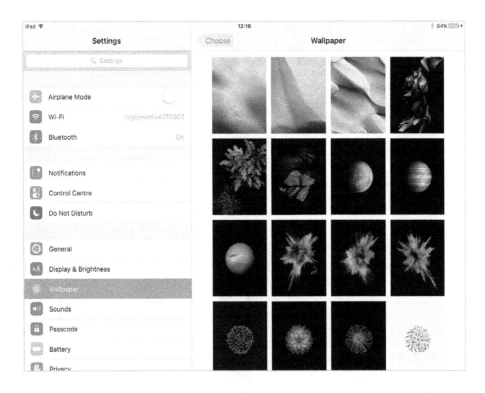

So far so good. What do you do though, if you don't like any of the supplied wallpapers? This leads us to your second option; use one of your own images.

In the 'Choose a New Wallpaper' screen, you will see a Photos section at the bottom – this lets you choose images from the Photos app.

You can select from default folders such as All Photos and Screenshots, plus any other folders you have created yourself. Selecting a picture is the same as for the Dynamic and Stills collections – tap the one you want and it will open in a full-screen preview.

At the bottom, you'll see the same options to set it as Lock Screen, Home Screen, and Set Both.

You can also set a picture as wallpaper directly from the Photos app. Open the app and select a picture by tapping it. Then tap the Options ⬆ button at the top-right of the screen. This opens a new screen that offers a 'Use as Wallpaper' option as shown in the image below:

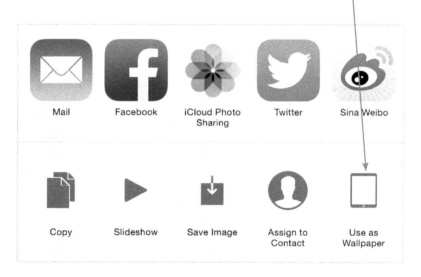

Note that pictures not supplied with the iPad will probably have the wrong dimensions for wallpaper. If this is the case, you'll see a 'Move and Scale' message at the top of the picture. Use your fingers to crop and adjust the picture by dragging it to the left or right, up or down, stretching to zoom in and pinching to zoom out. When you have it as you want it, set it as wallpaper as already described.

Finally, you can also import pictures to your Photos app, either from your computer via iTunes, or from the Internet via the Safari web browser, and set them as wallpaper in the same way as described above. We explain how to import pictures in Chapter 9.

Date & Time

Your iPad offers a number of date and time related functions, e.g. a clock, a calendar, reminders, as indeed do many third-party apps available from the App Store. For these to work correctly, it is essential that the date and time, and your time zone, are correctly set.

The procedure is:

1. Open the Settings app

2. Tap General and then tap Date & Time

3. Choose between a 24- or 12-hour clock by tapping the 24-Hour Time button switch to On

4. Turning 'Set Automatically' on will set the date and time via any network the iPad is connected to

5. If the iPad is not connected to a network, or you would rather do it manually, disable Set Automatically and then tap Time Zone

6. Using the keyboard, enter the name of a nearby city and your iPad will calculate the correct time zone from your location

7. Underneath Time Zone, tap the date and time (shown in blue)

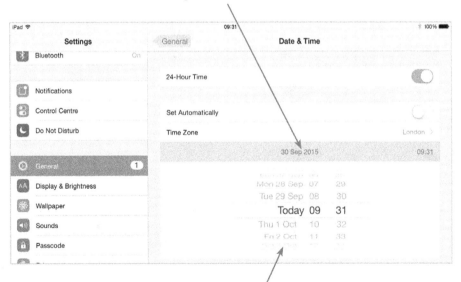

8. Spin the wheel controls to set the day, hour and minute

Sounds

The purpose of some apps is keep you informed of various types of information as it comes in. News headlines, emails, text messages, and weather updates are typical examples. To bring these to your attention, the apps use alerts, both visual and audible.

Just using your iPad also generates sounds, e.g. locking/unlocking the device and tapping keys on the virtual keyboard. Usually, you will be quite happy to hear these sounds as they do add another dimension to your use of the device. However, you may find a particular sound to be inappropriate, impractical or simply not to your liking. If so, you can change it in the iPad's settings.

Tap the Settings app on the Home screen and then tap Sounds. The Sounds options screen will open as shown below:

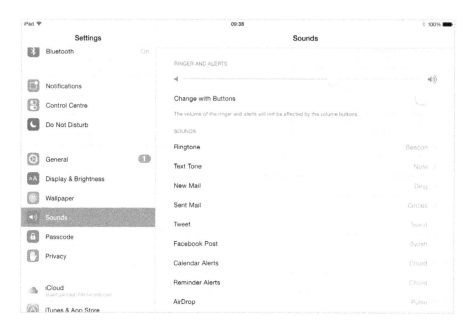

Right at the top is an option that lets you set the volume of ringers and alerts with the volume control buttons – by default, this is turned off. If you turn the setting on, you will effectively have a universal volume control that controls all the iPad's sounds. With it off, you can have music playing at one level, for example, and alerts set at a different level.

In the Sounds section below, you can change the sound associated with the iPad's various alerts. Just tap the alert, e.g. New Mail, and you'll be presented with a list of available sounds. Tapping each sound gives you a preview and also selects it. You'll also see options to disable the sounds made by locking/unlocking your iPad, and the clicks made by tapping the keyboard's keys.

Privacy

Many of the apps you use on your iPad, both Apple and third-party, share information between themselves. For example, the Mail app can access the contents of your Contacts app in order to facilitate the quick addressing of emails.

When you first run a third-party app that wants to use data from another app, it will request your permission to do so. If you grant it, the app will continue to use that data without further requests.

Your iPad provides a feature called Privacy that not only allows you to monitor exactly what data is being accessed by third-party apps but to also revoke any permissions previously granted.

1. Open the Settings app and tap Privacy

2. You'll see a list of apps and services that provide data. Apps include Contacts, Calendar and Photos, and services include your Twitter and FaceBook accounts (assuming you have them set up)

3. To see what third-party apps are accessing these apps and services, tap the relevant entry

4. If you want to deny an app in the list access to data from other apps and services, tap the switch at the right to the Off position

Accessibility

For users with disabilities that make it difficult to use the iPad, the device provides a range of accessibility features that can help considerably. You can access the settings for all these features by opening the Settings app and going to General > Accessibility.

There are quite a few options here and we'll briefly run through the most important ones to see what they offer.

For the visually impaired:

VoiceOver

VoiceOver is a screen reader that reads aloud, providing an audible description of everything that is happening on the iPad. For example, it tells you the name of someone who is calling, speaks the letter being touched on the keyboard, what app your finger is on, and helps you navigate the device. The pitch, speaking rate, language, and dialect of the voice can be altered if necessary.

A VoiceOver feature called the Rotor provides help specific to the navigation of web pages and documents.

Your iPad is fully compatible with many refreshable Braille displays. You can synchronize a Bluetooth wireless Braille display to read VoiceOver output. Also, Braille displays with input keys can be used to control your device when VoiceOver is turned on.

Be aware that when you activate VoiceOver, the gestures used to control your iPad will change – you'll get a warning message pop up on the screen about this. Also, some VoiceOver features are on by default and others are off. If you decide to use VoiceOver, go through the various settings to make sure you get the best out of it.

Zoom

The iPad's Zoom feature is a built-in magnifier that works wherever you are in the device. Double-tapping with three fingers instantly zooms in 200 per cent, and you can adjust the magnification between 100 and 500 per cent.

While you're zoomed in, you can still use all the usual gestures to navigate your device. Plus, Zoom works with VoiceOver to help you both see and hear what's happening on the iPad.

Invert Colors

This feature simply turns black to white and vice versa, thus increasing contrast so that content is easier to distinguish.

Speech

If you find it difficult to read text on your iPad, Speak Selection can help by reading your email, messages, web pages and books to you.

Select text in any application, tap Speak, and the selected text is read aloud. You can adjust the voice's language and speaking rate, and have words highlighted as they're being read.

Larger Text

Larger Text lets you increase font size so making it easier to read. By dragging a slider, you can select any of 12 predetermined steps, each of which increases the size of the text.

For those with hearing problems, the iPad offers:

Hearing Aids

The Hearing Aids feature makes it possible to use compatible, Bluetooth equipped, hearing aids with your iPad. The hearing aid settings can be managed with your device.

Subtitles & Captioning

When enabled, this feature displays captions at the bottom of the screen, so you can read what's being said. This is useful if you are watching a video in a noisy environment, for example. However, Subtitles and Captioning only works if the video being watched supports the technology behind it.

You can choose from three built-in display styles, or create one of your own design (font, text size and color, background, etc).

Mono Audio

People with hearing problems may miss part of a stereo recording when using headphones. This is because stereo recordings usually have distinct left- and right-channel audio tracks.

The Mono Audio feature compensates by playing both audio channels in both ears and letting the user adjust the balance for greater volume in either ear.

For those with physical problems, the iPad offers:

Switch Control
Switch Control lets you control your iPad with a single switch, or multiple switches. These can be in the form of buttons, leaf, sip, puff, or even eye-blink switches. The switches connect wirelessly to the device and are positioned where you can easily activate them.

There are several ways in which to perform actions such as selecting, tapping, dragging, typing, and even freehand drawing. The basic technique is to use a switch to select an item or location on the screen, and then use the same (or a different) switch to choose an action to perform on that item or location.

There are three basic methods:

● **Item scanning (default)** – highlight items on the screen until one is selected

● **Point scanning** – use scanning cross-hairs to pick a screen location

● **Manual selection** – move from item to item on demand

Whichever method you use, when you select a single item (rather than a group), a menu appears so you can choose how to act on the selected item (tap, drag, or pinch, for example).

You can adjust the behaviour of Switch Control in a variety of ways to suit your needs and style.

AssistiveTouch
AssistiveTouch is a very useful application for those with impaired physical and motor skills. It enables the user to activate multi-touch gestures such as pinch-to-zoom, to trigger hardware features such as the volume and Home buttons, and even rotate the screen or take a screenshot – all with one finger.

The user can also employ a compatible adaptive accessory (such as a joystick) together with AssistiveTouch to control their iPad.

Accessibility Shortcut
This enables a number of the accessibility features to be activated by triple-pressing the Home button. Specifically, these are: VoiceOver, Invert Colors, Greyscale, Zoom, Switch Control and AssistiveTouch.

CHAPTER 5

Apps

In Chapter 5, we take a look at the business end of your iPad – its programs, or apps as they are more commonly known. We explain what the pre-installed apps do, show how to use the App Store to get more apps, and how to keep your apps updated.

We also see how to organize your apps so as to make the most efficient use of the iPad.

What is an App?

By itself the iPad is just a piece of hardware – beautifully designed and superbly constructed – but still just a piece of hardware. To do something useful, it requires instructions.

On a computer, these instructions are provided by software programs, most of which are highly complex, large in size (which means they can take a long time to install and configure), and require a considerable amount of system resources to run. Computer software can also be extremely expensive.

The app is the tablet equivalent of computer software. However, due to the power and system resource restraints placed on tablets by their reliance on battery power and small physical size, the software used on them needs to be similarly restricted in terms of power and resource requirements.

Thus, in general, apps for tablets are much more streamlined than their computer equivalents. They are small in size, quick to download and install, and very inexpensive. The downside is that currently, they provide limited options and are restricted to relatively simple tasks.

Having said that, as tablets become more powerful (an iPad Air 2 is twice as powerful as it's predecessor), the apps used on them will be capable of doing a great deal more.

An important feature of apps is that, in general, they do not interact with each other. As a result, the chances of having your iPad infected with viruses and malware are much less than with a computer running a Windows operating system.

Furthermore, with regard to the content created when using apps, this is saved within the app rather than to a file structure as found on computers. Also, this content is saved automatically as it is created, or edited – the user does not need to save it manually.

iPads are supplied with a number of pre-installed apps that provide basic functionality, such as email (the Mail app), an Internet browser (the Safari app) and the Camera app. To increase the capability of your iPad you can, of course, download other apps from the App Store as we'll see later.

For now though, we'll take a brief look at the pre-installed apps:

Pre-installed Apps

When you switch on the iPad, the icons you see on the Home screen are the pre-installed apps supplied with the device.

Apps pre-installed on your iPad

These are:

App Store – this is basically a link that opens Apple's App Store from where you can download apps to your iPad. Many of these are free, others need to be purchased. Note that you will need an Internet connection.

Mail – this app lets you send and receive email on your iPad. It is easy to set up and, if you already have an email account, you can quickly add it to the app.

iTunes Store – this app takes you to the iTunes Store from where you can download music, movies, TV programs, etc.

Safari – essentially a 'lite' version of the web browser found on Apple Macs, Safari is your portal to the Internet. Like most apps, it has a relatively sparse set of features but is still perfectly adequate for most users.

Messages – for those of you who like to send text messages, the Messages app can be used to send text, pictures and videos to and from other Apple devices; namely iPads, iPhones, iPod Touches and Apple Mac computers.

Music – an important app for many people, the Music app is used to play music on your iPad. You can upload music to the iPad from your computer via iTunes, or download it directly from Apple's iTunes Store.

Clock – by default, the Clock app shows the current date and time in your location. You can also view the time in any other country. Other functions include an alarm, a stopwatch and a timer.

Calendar – typical of all digital calendars, the Calendar app lets you make and store appointments etc. By synchronizing the app with iCloud, your appointments can also be viewed and edited on other Apple devices.

Photos – this app not only lets you view pictures, it provides some useful editing functions as well. Pictures can be organized in albums and shared using iCloud.

Camera – the Camera app lets you use the iPad's front- and rear-facing cameras. With them, you can take pictures and videos both to keep in albums and to share online with social media.

Contacts – this app is an electronic address book in which to store the contact details of the people in your life. Entries can be accessed and used by other apps such as Mail.

Reminders – a very useful app, Reminders ensures you don't forget to do things. It can also be used to create to-do lists. Reminders can be accessed on all your Apple devices via iCloud.

FaceTime – the FaceTime app lets you make video calls to other iPad users and to people who have an iPhone, iPod Touch or Apple Mac computer. The app utilizes the front-facing camera.

Maps – with the Maps app, you can view specific regions from around the globe, find places, and get directions from one location to another. It also has a feature called Flyover that gives a birds-eye view of many interesting places.

Podcasts – a podcast is basically a subscription-based audio or video file that is broadcast over the Internet – the iPad's Podcasts app is used to play these files. Podcasts are an increasingly popular form of communication.

Videos – the Videos app stores television programs and movies that you download from the iTunes Store. It also lets you play them – just tap on one to begin playback.

Notes – a very useful app for jotting down things that pop into your head so you don't forget them. This app is much improved in iOS 9 and has many new features, such as being able to create bulleted lists and embed documents.

Settings – the Settings app is your way into the iPad. With it, you can change the default settings for most apps, set up email, configure network connections, customize your iPad, and much more.

iBooks – this app lets download books to your iPad from Apple's iBooks Store. Note that while it is very similar to Amazon's Kindle app, it cannot be used to download books from Amazon.

Tips – as the name suggests, the Tips app provides tips and tutorials on how to get the best out of the iPad. These are automatically updated on a regular basis.

Game Center – the Game Center is a central location for all things to do with gaming. Preview and download the latest games, play against yourself or challenge friends.

News – new in iOS 9, the News app lets you access stories from a number of local news sources. You can save sources as favorites, search for specific stories and save stories for reading later on.

Find My Friends – Find My Friends displays the location of your friends on a map (assuming they choose to share it). Your friends will also need to be using the app on their devices.

Find iPhone – for people who also have an iPhone, this app lets you see the location of your iPhone on a map. And with the Lost Mode feature, you don't just see where your device is, you can track where it's been.

iCloud Drive – With iCloud Drive, you can safely store all your presentations, spreadsheets, PDFs, images and any other kind of document in iCloud, and access them from your iPhone, iPad, iPod touch, Mac or computer.

The App Store

In all likelihood, it probably won't be long before you want to increase the capabilities of your iPad by downloading a new app. Unlike Windows computers that let you download programs from virtually anywhere (together with the attendant risk of also downloading viruses and malware), you have only one place to go with regard apps for your iPad.

This is the App Store. Not only does it offer a huge range of apps that cover every conceivable purpose, you can browse and download from it safe in the knowledge that it is just about the most secure site on the Internet. All apps in the store are stringently checked before they are offered for download. Also, the very nature of apps, most of which are basically self-contained programs that do not access the outside world, makes them inherently safer than computer programs.

Accessing the Store
To access the App Store, tap the App Store icon on the Home screen. When it opens, you will see something similar to the image below:

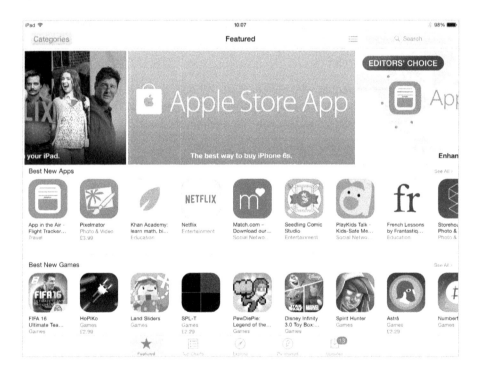

Browsing the App Store
At the top-left of the screen is a Categories button – tap this to reveal a list containing around 25 categories of apps. At the top-right is a button that opens your wish list. Next to that is a search box.

cont'd

Right at the bottom is a row of buttons. These include:

- **Featured** – tap this to open a page showing a range of featured apps. This includes sections for Best New Apps, Best New Games, Kids Apps & Games, Best New Game Updates and more

- **Top Charts** – on this page, you'll see scrollable sections that show the highest rated Paid, Free, and Grossing apps

- **Explore** – the Explore option lets you drill down by category – some of the apps shown are based on your geographical location

- **Purchased** – on this page, you will see all the apps you have bought from the App Store. If the app is on the iPad, you'll see an Open icon to the right – tapping this will open the app. If it has been downloaded at some point, either to your iPad or to a different device, but is not currently on your iPad, you'll see a ⬇ download icon – tap this to re-download and install the app

- **Updates** – we look at this on page 73

So, as you can see, the App Store provides a number of ways for you to find the app you are looking for, or indeed just have a look at what's available.

If you are looking for something specific and know its name, the search box is the quickest way to locate it. Otherwise, tap Explore and drill down through the various categories.

Reviewing & Installing Apps

As you're browsing, you'll notice a box to the right of each app in which is either the word GET or a price. GET indicates the app is free – tap it and you will now see INSTALL.

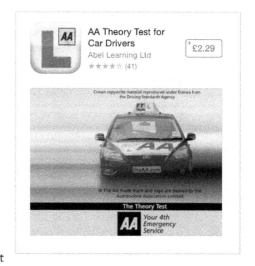

The iTunes Store login window will pop up asking for your account password. Enter it and then tap OK to start the download and installation procedure.

If you see a price in the box, this is what the app costs. As there is money involved, you may wish to get more detailed information about the app before shelling out.

cont'd

To do this, tap on the app to open the Details and Reviews screen as shown in the example below:

Right at the top, you'll see how the app has been rated by other users. For many apps, there will be a series of thumbnail images showing the app in action – scroll to the right to see them all. Below, will be a description of the app and other information such as its version history.

Tap the Reviews button to read the reviews left by people who have bought the app. If you decide you want it, tap the price box.

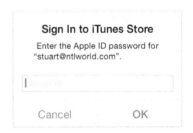

This leads to the BUY box, which in turn opens the 'Sign In to iTunes Store' screen. Enter your Apple password and press OK. The app will be charged to the credit card registered to your account, and then downloaded to your iPad and automatically installed.

Go to the end of your Home screen (the last one if you have more than one) and you'll see the icon for your new app.

Updating Your Apps

Many apps undergo development that enhance and extend their functionality and performance. This is important because the technology behind apps is fast-moving – developers who don't keep up are soon left behind. So if you want the apps on your iPad to be current and provide top-notch features, you need to update them periodically. There are two ways you can do this – manually and automatically. We'll start with the manual method:

When updates are available for your apps, you will see a red badge at the top-right of the App Store icon that shows the number of available updates. Open the App Store and, at the bottom of the screen, you'll see the Updates button is showing the same number.

Tap the Updates button and on the screen that opens, you'll see the apps for which updates are available. Tap Update All at the top-left, or update them individually with the separate UPDATE buttons.

The automatic method is much easier. Open the Settings app and go to iTunes & App Store. In the Automatic Downloads section, simply tap the Updates button to On.

That's all there is to it. From now on, your iPad will download and install app updates as and when they become available.

Managing Your Apps

Your iPad starts you off with over 20 apps and, in time, you will no doubt install many more. To be able to use your iPad efficiently, all these apps need to be organized so you can find them quickly. This may be difficult if you have them randomly scattered across several home screens.

Moving Apps
One of the first things you can do is rearrange the order of your apps. To move one, press and hold it until it begins to wiggle and then simply drag it to where you want it to go. Release it and then tap the Home button.

You can rearrange the Dock apps in this way as well. Furthermore, you can change the default Dock apps by dragging the originals off the Dock and then dragging different apps to the vacated spaces, It is also possible to add another two to the default four making a total of six.

If you don't want a particular app on your Home screen at all but don't want to go the lengths of actually deleting it, you can place it on a secondary home screen where it is out of the way. Simply drag the app to the right-hand edge of the screen and a secondary home screen is created automatically – release the app there. This is one way of dealing with the default Apple apps that you don't use.

You can create up to 11 home screens on the iPad and have 20 apps on each, plus six on the Dock. According to the maths, this makes it possible to have a maximum of 226 apps on your iPad. However, by creating app folders as we see below, it is possible to have even more.

App Folders
The ability to create folders in which to place your apps provides another method of organizing your iPad. This feature can be used for various purposes. For example: grouping related apps under one icon, creating more space for apps, and making it easier to find particular apps.

Follow these steps to create a new folder:

1. Go to the home screen that contains one of the apps you want to include in the new folder

2. Press and hold the app until its icon begins to wiggle

3. Drag the app to the top of another app that you also intend to place in the folder. Then release it. Note that if the two apps are on different screens, you can drag from one screen across to the other

Your iPad will now create a new folder. Tap to open it and you'll see that it contains your two apps as shown on the next page.

The iPad will automatically give the folder a name based on the type of apps in it. This is demonstrated in the image on the right, which shows the Photo Booth app dropped onto the Photos app. The apps are both photography related so the iPad has named the folder Photography.

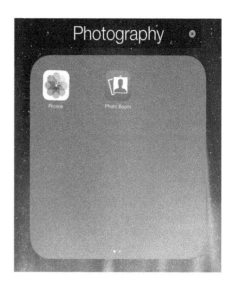

If you want to name the folder yourself, tap the X to the right of the name and the keyboard will open. Type the name and then tap Done. If you don't see the X, press and hold one of the app icons until they begin to wiggle – the X will now be visible.

You can add more apps by dragging them onto the folder's icon. Remove them by opening the folder and dragging them out. You can also rearrange the order of the apps within the folder by pressing until the icons wiggle and then dragging them to the new positions.

Finally, if you place more than nine apps in the folder, the 10th and above apps will be put on a new screen within the folder. Swipe right to access it.

Opening & Closing Apps

To open an app, just tap the app's icon – it couldn't be simpler. What isn't so straightforward is how to close it. You can press the Home button but this doesn't actually close the app, it just returns you to the Home screen – the app is still open, albeit in a state of suspension whereby it is using very little of the iPad's resources. The latter is an important concept to grasp as it means you don't need to close apps down at all. You can actually have any number of them running simultaneously without any noticeable performance hit on the iPad.

However, should you feel the need to do so for whatever reason, the way to close them is to double-press the Home button. This opens the multitasking interface (see page 21), which shows a mini representation of all open apps. To close one, just swipe it upwards.

Deleting Apps

When you've had a chance to play around with your iPad and see what the default apps do, it's quite likely that you'll decide some of them are superfluous to requirements, and are thus candidates for deletion. To do this, simply press and hold on the app until its icon begins to wiggle as previously described.

If the app can be deleted, an X will appear at the top-left of the icon – tap it to initiate the delete process. In the Delete window that opens, tap Delete – the app will be removed from the iPad.

However, not all apps can be deleted. With the default Apple apps supplied with the iPad, the X will not appear – this means these apps cannot be deleted. Similarly, if you create a folder that contains an Apple app, you will not be able to delete the folder until you take the app out of the folder.

Reinstalling Apps

You may at some point delete an app (due to lack of use, the need to reclaim storage space, etc) only to decide later that you would like it back. The App Store makes it easy to reinstall deleted apps. Open the Store and at the bottom of the screen, tap Purchased. Then, at the top, tap 'Not on This iPad'.

You will now see all the apps that you have installed and then deleted since your Apple account was created. At the right of each app, you will see a Cloud icon with a down-arrow. Just tap the icon to reinstall the app.

Switching Between Open Apps

You may sometimes need to use two or more apps to achieve a particular goal, and so being able to quickly switch between them will be handy. If you have a Pro, Air 2, or Mini 4 iPad, you can use the Split View feature as we explained on pages 22-23. If not, you can use the multitasking screen as we explained on page 21.

Another way is to use the four-finger gesture. Place four fingers on the screen of an open app and swipe left and right to switch between it and other apps.

CHAPTER 6

Getting Online

One of the biggest boons offered by tablets in general is the ability to use the Internet while on the move. Sure, this can also be done on a smartphone but the larger screen of a tablet enhances the experience enormously. In this chapter we show you how to connect your iPad to the Internet.

To use the Internet you will need a web browser and the iPad provides one of the best – the Safari app. This offers a good range of features and functions that, quite apart from browsing, also enables you to bookmark your favorite sites, get rid of irritating in-line ads, hide your browsing tracks and much more.

Types of Connection

Connecting your iPad to the Internet is done via a network, of which there are two types – Wi-Fi and Cellular. Accordingly, iPad's are supplied as either Wi-Fi only models or Wi-Fi/cellular models. While the former can only connect to Wi-Fi networks, the latter can connect to both types of network. If you're not sure which model you have, open the Settings app and look at the top of the left-hand column.

If you just see Wi-Fi, that's what you have. If you see a Cellular entry as well, then you have the cellular model. A lot of people are confused by the difference between the two so we'll clarify the issue here:

Wi-Fi
A Wi-Fi iPad can only connect to the Internet via a wireless, or Wi-Fi signal. These signals are produced by a device called a router that typically has a range of approximately 150 feet indoors and 300 feet outdoors.

Many homes have these routers installed as part of their broadband setup, and they are also widely found in public places such as airports, libraries and Internet Cafes. The latter are known as Wi-Fi hotspots and they enable people to use their iPads and smartphones while on the move.

The advantage of Wi-Fi is that if you use your iPad at home, your connection is free. Some public places offer free Wi-Fi hotspots but most don't, in which case you have to pay for the connection.

The disadvantage is if you are in an area where Wi-Fi is not available, you won't be able to access the Internet, send/receive email, and you'll find that any apps that rely on Internet access will not work.

Cellular
Cellular iPads, on the other hand, can connect to the Internet wherever there is cellular network coverage, in the same way that cell phones do. This is their big advantage and one that is much valued by people who travel a lot.

Furthermore, by installing a suitable app such as Skype (available from the App Store), a cellular iPad can also be used as a phone.

Cellular iPads are designed to access a large frequency spectrum. This means they will work well in most locations globally that offer a cellular service.

Needless to say of course, there is a downside – namely cost! Cellular iPads are considerably more expensive than the Wi-Fi models. Not only that, you will also need to pay for a data service plan. This is essentially the same as the plan you buy for your cell phone and is subject to the same data restrictions and costs.

Set Up a Wi-Fi Connection

Unlike cellular connections, Wi-Fi connections are not automatic – they have to be set up.

As soon as you initiate an action on your iPad that requires an Internet connection, e.g. opening the Safari web browser, the device will look for a Wi-Fi signal with which to make the connection.

Assuming this is the first time you've initiated such an action, your iPad will then present you with a list of the Wi-Fi networks it has found, i.e. that are within range of the device.

This gives you the following information:

- On the left is the name of the network, e.g. virginmedia0183048

- On the right, you may or may not see a padlock icon. If you do, it indicates the network is password-protected

- Next to this is the signal strength icon. The more bars, the stronger the signal, and thus the faster and more reliable the connection

Making a Connection

Tap the Wi-Fi network you want to join. If it requires a password, enter the password at the prompt and then tap Join at the top-right.

If the password is accepted, your iPad will connect to the network and, as an indication of this, you'll see the Wi-Fi network icon appear at the left of the Status bar. In the case of a commercial network that requires up-front payment, you will be asked to enter your name and credit card details before you are allowed to use the network.

Note that when you join a free network, henceforth, whenever your iPad is in range of that network, it will automatically login to it – you won't have to select it and enter the password every time.

cont'd

Connecting to Your Home Broadband

If you have a broadband Internet connection in your home and the setup includes a Wi-Fi router (as most do these days), you're all set for free Wi-Fi on your iPad:

1. Locate your router and look at the rear of the case

2. You'll see a SSID number, e.g. virginmedia123456 and a passphrase. Make a note of them

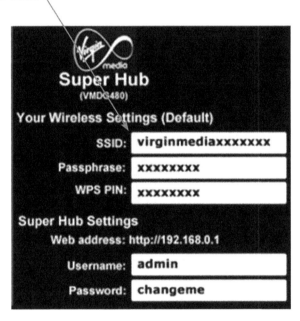

3. If you haven't set up a connection on your iPad yet, follow the procedure described on the previous page. When you see the dialogue box showing the list of available connections, choose the one that has the same name as the SSID number on the back of your router

4. Enter the passphrase in the password box and tap Join – job done

Now it may be that your broadband router is the outdated type that doesn't provide Wi-Fi. If this is the case, contact your Internet service provider (ISP) and ask them to send an engineer to update your router. They should do this free of charge.

With regard to SSID numbers, note that all Wi-Fi networks are given an identifying name – this is the Service Set Identifier, or SSID for short. A typical example is shown in step 2 above – virginmediaxxxxxxx – this enables you to differentiate between networks and connect to the one you want.

Safari Web Browser

Before you start browsing the Internet with the iPad, it will be as well to familiarize yourself with the app you'll use to do it – the Safari web browser. Tap Safari on the Home screen to get started.

The screenshot below shows Safari's main elements, plus the controls you will use to navigate both the Internet and individual web pages:

- **Forwards/Backwards** – tap the arrows to navigate between pages

- **Address/Search Box** – this is where you enter the address of a website you want to visit. It also doubles as a search box – simply enter your search term and tap Go on the keyboard

- **New Tab** – tap to open a new tab

- **Bookmarks** – this gives you access to your Bookmarks, Favorites and Reading List. You will also find options to manage them

- **Options** – these include sharing a web page via AirDrop, text message, email, Twitter or Facebook. There are also options to bookmark a page, add it to a reading list, add it to the Home screen, copy it, and print it

- **Tab View** – tap this to open a thumbnail list of all open tabs

Opening a Web Page

To open a web page in Safari, tap in the address/search box. The keyboard will open at the bottom of the screen allowing you to type the address.

After you have been using the browser for a while, you'll notice that Safari tries to predict the address based on what you have already typed in an attempt to speed things up. If it gets it right, stop typing and tap Go on the keyboard. If it gets it wrong, just ignore it and keep typing.

Predicted text (highlighted in blue)   Suggested web pages

Also, as you type, Safari will suggest pages it thinks are relevant to what you are entering in the address/search box – these appear below the box. The suggestions are also influenced by pages you have previously visited and past searches. Just tap one of the links to go to the page.

If you find this feature annoying or simply don't need it, you can turn it off in Safari's settings. Open the Settings app and go to Safari > Search Engine Suggestions. Tap the switch to Off.

When you finish a browsing session and close Safari, it will remember the last page visited. The next time you open the browser, it will open that page, the address of which will be in the address/search bar.

To clear the address/search box so you can enter a different address, just tap anywhere in the box. The address will be highlighted as shown above. Clear it by either tapping the X at the far-right of the box or by simply typing over it.

Viewing & Navigating Web Pages

Viewing and navigating a web page with a touchscreen tablet requires a different technique than the traditional computer/mouse combination. With a tablet, touch gestures are the order of the day and while they are not as precise as a mouse cursor it is, nevertheless, surprising just how effective they are.

- **Panning** – placing a finger on the screen and moving it left, right, up, and down enables you to move, or pan, the page. To move quickly, flick your finger – the faster you flick, the faster the page moves

- **Zooming** – due to the small screen size of tablets, zooming is a much more important issue than it is when browsing the Internet with a full-size computer monitor. Before you do though, try simply rotating the tablet so you are holding it in Landscape mode – this will increase the size of screen elements and may be all that's necessary

  If not, double-tap the area you want to zoom into. This may be an area of text, an image, or a form, and it will be magnified to the width of the screen. To zoom back out, double-tap again

  To zoom with more control, place two fingers on the screen and move them apart – this action zooms in. Pinching your fingers will zoom out. Note that you should place your fingers on the part of the screen you want to zoom into or out of

- **Move to the top** – if you are down at the bottom of a long page, rather than pan back up, just tap at the top of the screen – this action instantly takes you to the top of the page

- **Links** – web pages often contain links to this, that and the other. If you want to know where a link leads before actually going to it, press and hold the link. A small pop-up will appear and at the top will be the link's address

  Below, you will see a number of options one of which is Open. Below that is 'Open in New Tab'. Tap this and the link will open in a new tab – we'll see how to configure this option on the next page

Another option is Copy. Tap this and go to another app, such as Mail or Notes. Position the cursor, tap and then tap Paste. You can now save the link or email it, depending on the app you are using.

Browsing With Tabs

Before the concept of tabbed browsing was conceived, an Internet browsing session could be a somewhat painful experience that involved opening numerous pages, each in its own window, and constant use of the back and forward buttons. Losing your starting point, i.e. the original page, was very easy to do. Furthermore, all these open windows placed a considerable load on the computer's resources that could reduce it to a crawl.

The introduction of tabs has resolved these issues and made it possible to have any number of pages open simultaneously, and to instantly switch between them without ever touching the back and forward buttons. At the same time, the original page can be kept open in case you need to go back to it.

Opening Tabs

Opening a tab in Safari is very simple and can be done in two ways:

- **The Tab Button** – at the far top-right of the browser window, you will see an icon in the shape of a cross – tap this to open a new tab. All open tabs are shown on the Tab bar, which is situated just below the address/search box, and can be accessed from the bar

- **Links** – on the previous pages we saw how there are several options with regard to opening web page links, such as Copy and Open. Another of these options is 'Open in New Tab'

When you select this option, the page is loaded in the tab but the current page is kept in the foreground – just tap the new tab to switch to the new page. However, if you'd rather go to the new tab automatically, you can configure this in Safari's settings:

1. On the Home screen, tap the Settings app

2. Tap Safari on the left-hand side and then on the right, tap the 'Open New Tabs in Background' option to Off

Tab View

As we have seen, you can view your open tabs and switch from one to the other from the Tab bar. However, this is not ideal as you can't actually see what's on each tab.

Safari's Tab View provides the solution. Tap the Tab View ⬜ icon at the top-right of the screen and you will be presented with a thumbnail view of all the tabs currently open in Safari:

You'll now be able to see what's on the pages, making it much easier to select the one required – just tap on the thumbnail to go to it. Note that multiple tabs from the same site are grouped together, i.e. stacked, as shown above.

iCloud Tabs

You are sitting at home reading a web page on your iPad. However, you have to leave to take someone to the hospital before you can finish the page. Wouldn't it be handy if you could just pick up where you left off with your iPhone while waiting at the hospital?

Well, with iCloud Tabs you can – any Safari tabs left open on one of your Apple devices will be accessible on all the others. However, the devices must all be signed in to the same iCloud account – we explain how to sign in to iCloud on page 189. To test it is working, open some tabs in Safari on your iPad. Then open Safari on your other device, and tap the Tab View icon. At the bottom, below the thumbnails, you will see a list of all the tabs open on the iPad. Just tap on one to open it.

Viewing Articles With Safari Reader

Many web pages these days contain a number of elements that can get in the way of the page's content. Typical examples are images, videos and adverts that contribute nothing worthwhile to a site's content. Then there is all the stuff necessary to make the site work such as sidebars, menus, links, search boxes and buttons. As a result, it is often surprisingly difficult to find and read a site's content. A solution provided with your iPad is Safari Reader. When activated, all that extraneous clutter is stripped away leaving just the article and any related images on the page. Reader is also useful for getting rid of those in-line advertising links that open in pop-up windows.

However, Reader doesn't work on all pages. Usually, this is when a page has two or more articles. In this case, you need to tap an article link to open it in a new window. You will then see the Reader icon appear to the left of the address bar.

Tap the icon and all those banner ads, unrelated images, menus, etc, will disappear as we see below in the Safari Reader view of this web page

While in Reader mode, you will notice an aA icon at the far-right of the address bar. Tap it to open a window that offers options for changing the font and font size, and a choice of background colors – white, black, sepia and gray.

Bookmarks & Favorites

The Internet is so vast that finding a useful page is a task that can take a long time and involve a lot of searching. So, having found such a page, it makes sense to ensure you can find it again, and quickly, should you ever need to.

This is where bookmarks come in. They allow you to save a link to pages you visit often, or might need to access again at some point. Favorites are simply bookmarks that are placed on the Favorites Bar at the top of the browser window. From here, they can be instantly accessed, i.e. they are your favorite bookmarks.

Creating a Bookmark

Bookmarking a page with Safari is simple:

1. Navigate to the required page in Safari

2. Tap the Options button at the left of the address/search bar

3. From the Options menu, tap Add Bookmark

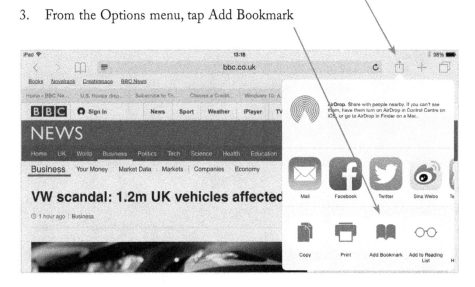

4. The bookmark is automatically named with the title of the page. However, this is usually long-winded so you may prefer to name it yourself. If so, tap the X at the right of the name to delete it and then enter the name you'd prefer

5. Under the Name box, you'll see an option called Location. Tap this and you'll be able to choose between saving the bookmark as a favorite (favorite bookmark) or as an ordinary bookmark. Make your choice and then tap Save (or Done on the keyboard)

cont'd

Opening Favorite Bookmarks

Your favorite bookmarks are placed in a bar at the top-left of the browser window for immediate access. Just tap on one to open it.

Another way is to tap the + icon at the top-right to open a new tab – you will now see large icons of all your favorites in a browser window. Yet another way is to tap once in the address/search bar – this opens a pop-up window showing the same large icon view of the favourites.

Opening Bookmarks

To open an ordinary bookmark, tap the Bookmarks icon at the left of the address/search bar.

In the window that opens, you'll see your bookmarks below the Favorites and History folders. Just tap one to open it.

The History folder contains a chronological record of every site you have visited over a period of several days.

This can be useful if you forget to bookmark a page – just scroll through the list of visited web pages until you find the one you are looking for.

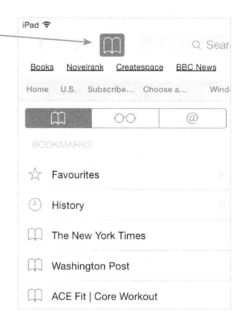

Reading Lists

Every now and then you'll come across an interesting web page that you don't have time to finish reading. Or you may be looking for information on a certain topic for later perusal.

Whichever, Safari has it covered in the form of its Reading List feature. This works by downloading the page to the iPad so you can read it at your leisure. Furthermore, because it is stored on the iPad, you do not need to be connected to the Internet to do so.

Add a Page to Your Reading List
Having found a page you want to save for reading later, the way to add it to your reading list is:

1. Tap the Options ⬆️ button at the right of the address/search bar

2. In the pop-up window that opens, tap 'Add to Reading List'

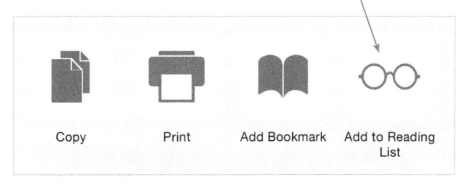

| Copy | Print | Add Bookmark | Add to Reading List |

Accessing Your Reading List
When you are ready to read some of the pages in your reading list, access the list by:

1. Tapping the Bookmarks icon at the left of the address bar

2. Tapping the Reading List icon (shaped like spectacles). You will now see a list of all the pages saved. Tap any item to open the page

3. At the bottom of the list, you will see 'Show Unread' and 'Show All'. The latter shows all the pages in your list; the former just the ones that haven't been opened yet

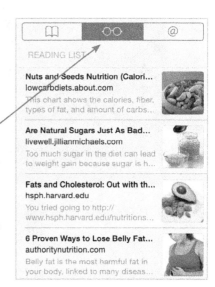

Private Browsing

If you are security conscious, you may want to take a look at your iPad's Private Browsing feature. This lets you browse the Internet without leaving any traces of what you have been doing. When in Private Browsing mode, Safari doesn't save any website data so there is no way for anyone else to see what you've been up to.

For example:

- Web pages are not stored in Safari's History list

- Text and images are not stored

- Search box entries are not saved

- AutoFill is disabled

- Web pages cannot be seen on your other iOS devices via iCloud tabs

To activate Private Browsing:

1. Open Safari and tap the Tab View icon at the far top-right

2. In the window that opens, tap Private

3. You will now see the screen below saying you are in Private Browsing Mode. Tap the + button at the top-right to open a new tab

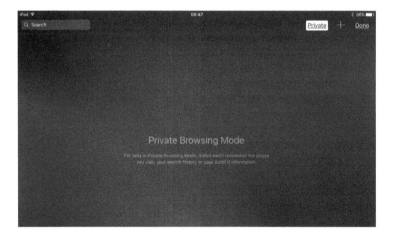

4. The top of the browser turns dark indicating you are now in Private Mode. From this point, you are browsing in complete privacy

5. When you want to return to normal browsing, tap the Tab View icon again, tap Private and then tap Done

Searching With Safari

As we've already mentioned, the address box also doubles as Safari's search box. You can use it to search the entire Internet, or just a single web page.

Search the Internet

Tap in the box to bring up the keyboard and type in your search term. By default, the search is done via Google and you will see four suggestions listed below the search box. If any of these are relevant, tap to open the page.

If not, tap Go on the keyboard to open a full list of Google search results.

Search a Web Page

Open the required web page, tap in the address box to bring up the keyboard and type in your search term. At the bottom of the list of results, you will see a section entitled 'On This Page'. This will show your search term and the number of matches the search has found (you may have to hide the keyboard to see this).

On This Page

Find "taliban"   2 matches

Tap the search term and you will be taken to the first occurrence of the word; it will be highlighted in yellow.

The move came after Russia's parliament granted President Vladimir Putin authorization to use military force in the multi-layered conflict and capped a speedy effort by Russia in recent weeks to bolster the government of Bashar al-Assad.

By Andrew Roth and Daniela Deane · 33 minutes ago

Refugees play at a shelter. (Adam Berry for the Po

U.S. coalition troops sent to Afghan city to help fight the Taliban

For the first time, coalition officials publicly confirmed that they are actively involved in boosting Afghan troops in Kunduz, a city seized by the Taliban a few days ago.

For some refugees, Zumba classes; for others, a night or the streets

Germany is having trouble housing the 527,0(asylum seekers that have made it to the coun so far this year.

‹ › 1 of 2 matches   🔍 taliban   ⊗ Done

At the bottom-left of the page, you will see Next and Previous arrows that take you to other instances of the word. When you are finished, tap Done at the bottom-right.

cont'd

A new feature in iOS 9 provides another way of searching a web page. This is called 'Find on Page' and it works as follows:

1. Open the web page

2. Tap the Options button at the right of the address bar

3. In the bottom section of the Options menu, scroll across to the right until you see 'Find on Page'

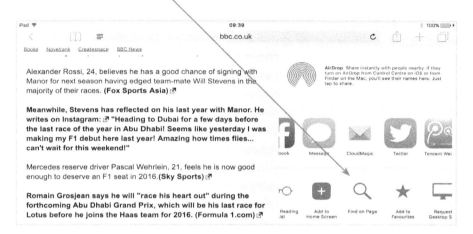

4. Tap Find on Page

5. The keyboard opens with a searchbox at the top-right.

6. Enter your search term and press the Search button. If the feature finds a match on the page, it will move to it and highlight it in yellow as we see above. At the top-left of the keyboard, you will see the number of matches found – if it is more than one, there will also be Previous and Next arrows that let you select them as required

Change the Default Search Engine

Your iPad comes with Google as the default search provider and you will probably be quite content with this. However, should you prefer to use a different search engine, you do have a choice.

Open the Settings app and go to Safari. At the top-right, you'll see Search Engine in the Search section. Tap this to open the options window:

Tap the search engine of your choice. Note that Baidu is a Chinese search engine, while DuckDuckGo is a relatively new search engine that puts privacy first and, as such, does not store IP addresses, does not log user information, and uses cookies only when needed. As a result, targeted advertising and skewed search results are largely eliminated.

Search by Voice Command

On pages 31-32, we took a look at Siri – the iPad's voice-controlled personal assistant. One of the many ways this feature can be used is to conduct Internet searches. Simply tell it what you are looking for and it will do its best to oblige. Some typical examples are:

- **Conducting a full Internet search** – e.g. 'search the web for world cup 2014', or 'search the internet for origins of apache indians'

- **A more specific Internet search** – e.g. 'world series baseball'

- **Searching with a specified search engine** – e.g. 'bing gold prices'

How you phrase the search is not critical as long as your meaning is clear.

When you are looking for a business or service, Siri uses data provided by Yelp. For example, you can locate restaurants by criteria such as cuisine, price, location, etc. It will also give you specific details of the restaurant including pictures, rating, prices, and reviews.

If you add a qualifier such as good, e.g. 'good thai takeaway', Siri will sort the results by their rating.

AutoFill

Many sites these days require you to create an account – this will include personal details such as your home and email addresses, phone number, etc. To log in to these accounts, you'll need to enter a password. Then there is online shopping, which requires you to enter your credit card details.

To save having to constantly enter this type of information, Safari provides a feature that can speed things up considerably – it is called AutoFill. When enabled, AutoFill does the work for you by automatically entering the requested information in the various fields (it takes the info from your contacts profile) – all you have to do is tap a button.

To set up AutoFill:

1. If you haven't already done so, create a contact for yourself in the Contacts app. Include all the information you are likely to need online

2. Tap the Settings app to open it

3. Go to Safari > AutoFill

4. Tap 'Use Contact Info' to On

5. Tap 'My Info' and then select your contact profile

From now on, when you tap a text field in a web page, the keyboard will open as normal but with the addition of an AutoFill option at the top-left as shown above. Tap an email field for example, then tap AutoFill, and your email address will be entered automatically.

As we mentioned at the top of the page, you can also enable the automatic entry of usernames, passwords, and credit card info. Fairly obviously, however, there are security issues with these options, so you may wish to consider carefully before enabling them.

Privacy & Security on the Internet

The Internet is a dangerous place, particularly for the uninitiated or unwary. Not only is your privacy at risk but your wallet as well!

Things you need to be aware of include:

- **Phishing** – phishing is when a fake website purports to be something respectable, a well known corporation perhaps, in order to gain your trust. Having done so, it will ask you to enter personal details such as passwords and account numbers, and then relieve you of your money

- **JavaScript** – JavaScript is a programming language used in web sites to add useful applications. Generally, it's a good thing but in the wrong hands it can be used to compromize a user's computer

- **Pop-ups** – a pop-up is a little window that quite literally pops-up unexpectedly when you are browsing a site. They may contain an annoying advertisment or something useful such as a login page

- **Cookies** – a cookie is a text file that websites download to your device. They store information about your current browsing session; a typical example being a shopping cart. However, they can also be used to track what you are doing and serve up related ads

- **History List** – Safari keeps a chronological list of all the sites you visit, which can be useful should you need to find a certain site again. However, anyone snooping through the list will be able to see exactly what you've been up to on the Internet

If any of these concern you, open the Settings app and tap Safari. Go to the Privacy and Security section where you will see various options:

The 'Fraudulent Website Warning' setting lets you turn phishing protection on or off. By default, it is on and we suggest you leave it on.

'Block Cookies' is also enabled by default. However, if you visit certain types of site you may want to change this. Tap the setting and you will be able to choose from a number of options.

In the General section, you'll see that pop-ups are blocked by default. This can result in a considerable loss of functionality in many websites, so you may want to turn this off.

Tap Advanced and you'll be able to toggle JavaScript support on or off.

With regards the History List, tap 'Clear History and Website Data'. Then tap Clear – this removes your history, cookies and other stuff.

Alternative Browser Apps

Safari is a good app and offers most of what is required from a web browser. There are, however, a lot of other browsers available from the App Store. While you may find Safari adequate, it could be that one of the others provides a feature that you need which Safari doesn't have. Or, you may just want to try something different.

Whatever, some browser apps you can try include:

- **Google Chrome** – Chrome is a popular alternative for people who use Google services. For example, if you use Chrome on your Mac or PC and save bookmarks, the app can sync them across your devices. You can also sign into your Google account with the app and all your settings and preferences will be right there

- **Opera Mini** – Opera Mini is reckoned to be the fastest browser available. This does come at a price though, as many of the features found in other browsers have been sacrificed accordingly. However, if speed is what you need, the Opera Mini is the one to go for

- **Dolphin** – due to its support for gestures and the use of sidebars, Dolphin provides a more intuitive way of browsing the web. It offers many useful options that include a downloads manager, a choice of search engines, tab browsing and much more

- **Mercury Browser Pro** – Mercury takes the best bits of Safari and Chrome and rolls them up into one of the best browsers available. Features include ad blocking, social network integration, and excellent support for gestures. It will even sync bookmarks and data across all your devices with both Firefox and Chrome

- **Puffin** – the feature that really defines Puffin is its speed. From loading web pages to tabbing through menus, it's smooth and quick. There are also numerous add-ons to choose from, the ability to download files, and much more besides

- **Atomic** – Atomic is a highly flexible browser that allows the user to set up advanced privacy controls, choose from several color themes, activate an ad-blocker, customize the search engine bar, view the source of a web page, and more

CHAPTER 7

Communicating

In Chapter 7, we look at the various ways you can use your iPad to communicate with the world outside. Email is the main one and we show you everything you need to know in this respect – types of email account, how to set up an email account, and how to use the iPad's default email app, Mail.

Another popular method is messaging and we show how to use the Messages app to send text, pictures and video. The iPad also provides a FaceTime app that lets you make face-to-face video calls – we take a look at this and see how it works.

Email Accounts

As with any type of computer, before you can use your iPad for email, you must first set up an email account. This is very easy to do – if you currently use one of the popular email services such as iCloud, Gmail, Yahoo, etc, it's even easier as much of the work is already done for you – just a few taps is all it takes.

If you decide to use a different service, such as the one from your ISP, you will need to provide more information though.

Email Services and Protocols

The easy way to set up an account is to use one of the six preconfigured email services provided with your iPad. These are all web-based and use the IMAP protocol (except for Microsoft Exchange, which uses the MAPI protocol).

Your iPad knows how to connect to all these services – all you need to supply is the email address and account password. If, however, you don't use any of these services, you will have to supply more information.

Apart from the email address and account password, you will also need to provide the names of the incoming and outgoing mail servers, plus any security info required to send email. You will also need to specify if the account is POP or IMAP.

All this information will be available from your email service provider – just ask them for it and you'll be ready to go. However, before we go into the mechanics of setting up an email account, we'll explain the difference between the email protocols, POP and IMAP.

- POP (Post Office Protocol) – with POP, emails are stored temporarily on your Internet Service Provider's (ISP's) server. When you connect to the server, the messages are downloaded to your iPad and then deleted from the server

  The advantage of POP is that because all your emails are stored on the iPad, they can be re-read at any time without the need to reconnect to the server. The disadvantage is that they can only be viewed on the iPad to which they were downloaded

- IMAP (Internet Message Access Protocol) – IMAP essentially works the other way. Messages are not downloaded to your iPad (although it may seem as though they are). They are actually stored permanently on the ISP's server and you simply read them from there.

  The advantage with this method is that your email can be accessed via any device regardless of its location. The disadvantage is that in order to do so, an Internet connection is necessary

Setting Up an Email Account

Setting up an Email Account

Get started by tapping the Settings app on the Home screen. Then:

1. Go to Mail, Contacts, Calendars on the left of the screen. Then tap Add Account. You will see the list of email services shown below. These are the iPad's six preconfigured email services that we mentioned on the previous page

2. Lets say you want to use Aol. Tap the Aol link and a configuration screen will open. Here, you will enter a name for the account, the email address, an account password and a description for the account

3. Tap Next. Your iPad will look up the details you have just provided. Assuming they check out, the account is set up without further ado

4. Tap Save

However, if you want to use an email service not preconfigured with the iPad, such as the one provided by your ISP, you will need to select the Other option at the bottom of the list.

While the procedure is much the same, you will need to also specify whether the account is POP or IMAP, and provide incoming and outgoing mail server addresses. Contact your ISP if you don't have this information.

When you do:

1. Tap Other and then tap 'Add Mail Account'

2. Enter the account name, email address, password and description in the relevant boxes. Then tap Next

3. Specify the type of account by tapping POP or IMAP

4. Under 'Incoming Mail Server', enter the host name, the username and the password in the respective fields

5. Under 'Outgoing Mail Server', enter the host name in the Host Name box

6. Tap Save

Your iPad will now verify the settings and, when done, add the account to your Accounts list.

Receiving Email

Once an account is set up, incoming emails will be received by the Mail app. New mail will be indicated by a red badge at the top-right corner of the app – this shows the number of new messages.

Tap the Mail app and it will open as shown above. The Inbox will appear on the left of the screen showing a list of all your emails. Messages that you haven't read yet are marked with a blue dot.

To read a message, just tap on it – this will highlight it in grey, and on the right of the screen (assuming you are holding the iPad in Landscape mode), it will open in the message window.

As soon as you open the Mail app, it automatically checks for new mail – this is indicated by a 'Checking for Mail ...' message at the bottom of the Inbox. You can also initiate a manual check at any time by dragging downwards on the Inbox, holding it for a second or two and then releasing – it will spring back up – this action queries the server for any new messages.

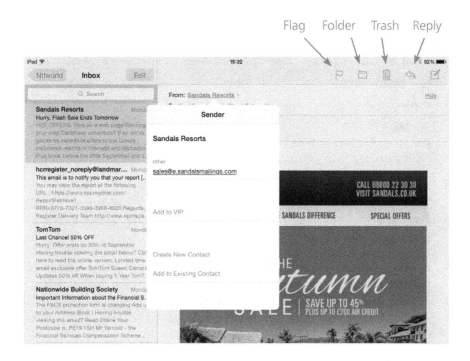

At the top of the message, tap the name or email address of the person sending the email. This opens a pop-up screen offering several options:

- Tap 'Add to VIP' to add the sender to your VIP inbox (see pages 108-109)

- Tap 'Create New Contact' to add the sender to your contacts list

- Tap 'Add to Existing Contact' to add the sender's email address to an existing contact

The icons at the top-right provide more options:

Flag – this offers various options. These include flagging messages with a red dot to highlight them, marking messages you have read as unread, moving messages to the junk folder, and requesting notification of replies

Folder – this opens a list of all the mailboxes associated with the email account. Tap one of the mailboxes to move the message to that mailbox.

Trash – tap the Trash icon to send the message to the Trash folder from where it can be subsequently restored or deleted permanently.

Reply – this provides three options: The first enables you to reply to the message, the second enables you to forward the message, and the third, Print, enables you to print the message.

Options for Receiving Email

Your iPad provides three options for the delivery of email to the device – Push, Fetch and Manual. This is an issue that affects battery life so you need to be aware of the differences between the three:

- **Push** – Push is the most active option as it automatically retrieves new messages as they arrive at your server. Choose Push if you want to receive your mail as soon as possible. Be aware though, that it makes a greater hit on the battery than either of the other options

- **Fetch** – with Fetch, your iPad will check for messages at set intervals of 15, 30, or 60 minutes. This means the app doesn't have to maintain a constant Internet connection, which in turn means battery power consumption is less than with Push

- **Manual** – with the Manual option, no email is received by the iPad until initiated by the user. Messages are received only when the Mail app is opened or when the screen is refreshed by dragging down on the inbox list. With regard to conserving battery charge, this is the best of the three options

To select the required option:

1. Open the Settings app and tap 'Mail, Contacts, Calendars'. Tap 'Fetch New Data'

2. If you want to use Push, tap to enable it

3. If you don't select Push, the iPad will use Fetch by default. In the Fetch section, select how often you want to check for mail

4. If you prefer to use the Manual option, this is also available from the Fetch settings

If you have more than one account, you can customize the settings for each one by tapping the relevant account – this brings up the Push, Fetch and Manual options.

As already mentioned, if you are concerned about data usage the recommended option is Manual.

Sending Email

Sending email messages with the Mail app is very straightforward. It may not provide some of the features and options found in more complex email clients such as Microsoft Outlook and Mozilla Thunderbird, but the ones it does provide are perfectly adequate as we will see.

Composing an Email Message

To write an email message on your iPad, tap the Mail icon on the Home page; it will open at the last received message. At the top-right of the screen tap the New Message ✎ icon. A new message window will open as shown below:

1. In the To: field, type the address. Alternatively, tap the + icon at the top-right to open your Contacts list from which you can select the recipient

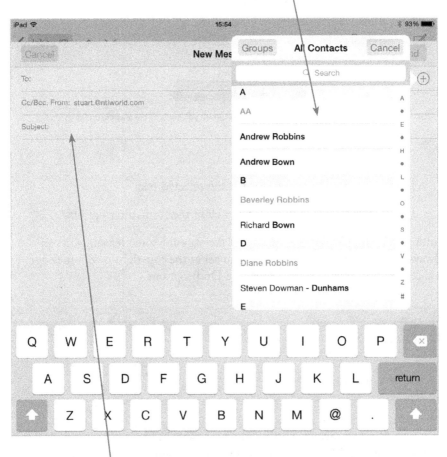

2. Tap in the Subject field and then type the subject

3. Tap in the Message field and then type your message

4. Tap Send at the top-right of the message window

Formatting Email Messages

We mentioned at the beginning of the previous page that, in general, the Mail app provides limited options compared to many email programs. This certainly applies to the formatting options on offer, which amount to Bold, Italics and Underline – nothing else.

If you want to use any of these options:

1. Tap and hold on the text to be formatted

2. In the menu bar that appears above, tap Select

3. Drag the blue selection handles to select all the text to be formatted

4. Tap B*I*U to reveal the Bold, Italics and Underline options

5. Tap the required option to format the selected text

6. Tap an empty part of the screen to close the formatting options

Note that if you have to stop writing a message for some reason, you can always finish it later. To do this, tap Cancel at the top-right of the message, which brings up Delete Draft and Save Draft options.

Tap Save Draft to save your incomplete message. When you are ready to finish it, navigate to the Mailboxes screen. Tap the relevant account and then tap the Draft folder. Finally, tap the message to open it.

Sending Pictures & Videos

Sometimes you may wish to send a picture or video with your email. The Mail app provides two ways to do this:

- Embed the image/video in the body of the email

- Send it as an attachment

Embed an image/video
To embed an image or video in an email with the Mail app, do the following:

1. Tap and hold in the email until a magnifying glass appears – in the magnifying glass, you'll see the cursor. Use your finger to drag the cursor to where the image or video is to be inserted

2. Lift your finger and you will see the set of options shown below:

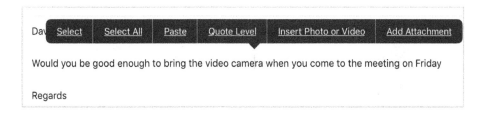

3. Tap 'Insert Photo or Video' – this will open a list of all the folders on your iPad that contain images and videos. Select a folder to reveal all the images /videos inside it

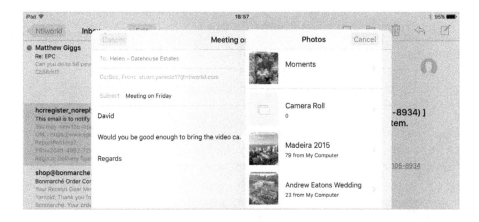

4. Tap the image/video to be embedded and then tap Use at the top-left of the screen

5. The image/video will be inserted at the place you specified with the cursor

cont'd

Send an Attachment

You can also attach files such as documents to your emails in iOS 9. There is, however, a proviso as we'll see. To do it, follow Steps 1 and 2 as detailed on the previous page to reveal the Options bar. At the far-right of the bar, you will see Add Attachment.

Tap it and you'll see the following:

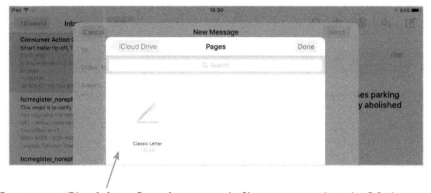

This is your iCloud drive. In order to attach files to an email in the Mail app, the file must be located in the Cloud – this is the proviso we mentioned. In the author's iCloud drive shown above, you can see that the drive contains a file. Tap the file and it will be attached to the email.

However, thanks to document provider extensions, you are not restricted to just iCloud – you can also attach files from other popular online storage services, such as Dropbox, Google Drive and OneDrive. Just download and install them from the App Store.

Once you have added another storage service, you will notice that the iCloud Drive button at the top-left has now changed to a Locations button. Tap it and then tap More to reveal and use the extra services you have installed.

Annotating Documents

A new feature in iOS 9 is Markup. This lets you annotate email attachments, such as images, PDF files and other types of document. Options include sketching, zooming, adding text, and adding signatures. Markup works with both incoming and outgoing attachments, which means that you can annotate the attachments you receive and those that you send.

Using Markup
Open the email that contains the document or image, and press and hold on it. This opens the Share menu where you will see a Markup and Reply button.

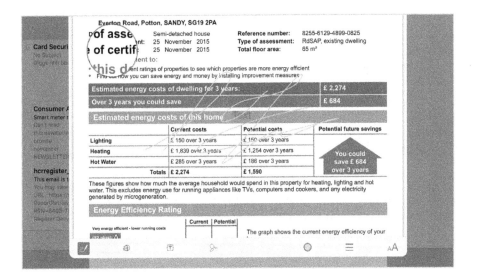

Tap the button and the image or document will open as we see above. At the bottom, you will see a toolbar that contains the markup tools. From left to right, these are:

- **Pen** – this lets you write and draw on the attachment

- **Magnifying glass** – move this around the document to zoom in

- **Text box** – this puts a resizable text box on the document that can be placed anywhere. Then use the keyboard to enter your text inside it

- **Add or remove signature** – this lets you create a permanent signature that can be used in all documents

- **Ink color** – this lets you select a range of colors for your markups

- **Line thickness** – choose from three possible line thicknesses

- **Text formatting** – options include font, text size, and justification

Managing Email

Create New Mailboxes

If you do a lot of emailing, it will be very helpful to organize your messages in related folders, or mailboxes. You can create any number of mailboxes for this purpose:

1. With the iPad held in Landscape mode, open the Mail app and tap the back arrow at the top-left of the screen

2. In the Accounts section at the bottom, tap the required account

3. Tap Edit

4. At the bottom, tap New Mailbox

5. Give the new mailbox a name and then tap Save

6. You will be returned to the folder list for that account where you will see the mailbox you have just created

Moving Messages

To move messages to your new mailbox, tap the required message in the Inbox to select it. Then tap the Folder button at the top-right of the screen – this opens the folder list for the account. Tap the new mailbox, or indeed any mailbox, and the message will be moved to it.

VIPs

iOS 9 provides an email feature called VIPs. This enables you to separate important email from the tidal wave of rubbish that no doubt washes inexorably into your inbox.

It works by creating a separate inbox called VIP to which all email that you classify as VIP mail is automatically copied. Note that these messages will still be in the main inbox. Furthermore, you will get a Notification Center alert whenever a message arrives from one of your VIPs (you can choose to stop this in Mail's settings if you wish).

To set up your VIP list:

1. Open the Mail app and go to the Mailboxes screen (tap the back arrow at the top-left of your inbox)

2. On the VIP line, tap the blue circle icon at the right-hand side

3. Tap 'Add VIP...' at the bottom – this opens your All Contacts list

4. Tap the contact you want to designate as a VIP. Repeat steps 3 and 4 to add further contacts

Another way to add to your VIP list is to open an email from someone you want as a VIP and then tap their name at the top of the message.

This opens a pop-up screen, where you will see a 'Add to VIP' option. Note that you can remove a VIP from the list in the same way.

At the bottom of the VIP list, you will see a VIP Alerts link. Tapping this takes you to the Notification Center settings where you can customize how you want the alert to appear and sound.

Any messages in your Inbox that have been copied to the VIP list will have a star icon at the left of the sender's name.

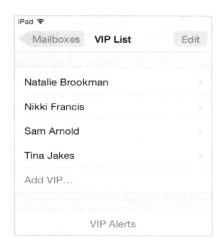

Thread Organization

By default, the Mail app groups messages by thread. This can be very useful as the original message and all the replies to it are grouped together, making it easy to follow the 'thread' of the conversation.

In your Inbox, messages that are part of a thread have a double arrow at the right of the date, as shown here.

However, while it can be convenient, not everyone likes the Thread Organization feature. If this applies to you, it can be turned off thus reverting to the standard chronological way of displaying messages.

To do it:

1. Open the Settings app

2. Tap Mail, Contacts, Calendars

3. In the Mail section, tap the 'Organize By Thread' switch to Off

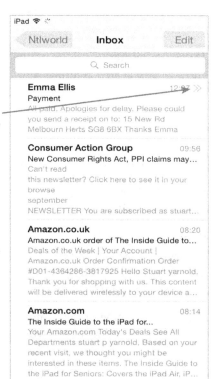

Emailing With Siri

If you don't want to get your hands dirty with the Mail app, give Siri a try; you will be surprised at how much you can do with it.

Reading Email

The following commands will enable you to read your emails:

- To display all unread emails, say 'open new mail'

- To display all emails from a specific account, say 'open new email from xxx account'

- To display emails from a specific person, say 'show all email from xxx'

- To display all emails in your Inbox, say 'show inbox'

Sending Email

To send a message, say 'email xxx' where xxx is the name of someone in your contacts list. If Siri recognizes the name, it will open a new email addressed to that person and then ask you what to put in the subject line. Then it will ask what message you want to send. Dictate your text and Siri will ask if you are ready to send it – just say yes or no. If you are not ready, you can make corrections at this point.

There is a quicker way to do all this though. Instead of going through the question and answer routine above, just give Siri all the information it needs to send the email in one go. Do it by using these keywords – 'email xxx', 'about', 'and say'.

In practice, this will look like:

> **email mike** (recipient) **about** (subject) **and say** (message text)

Siri will fill in everything automatically and then ask you if you want to send or cancel the email.

Replying to Email

You can also use Siri to reply to emails To do this, open the email, activate Siri and say 'reply'. Siri will ask what you want to say – dictate your text and say yes when asked if you are ready to send it.

These are just some of the commands you can use to control the Mail app with Siri – if you experiment, you will no doubt find there are many more.

Messaging

We've all seen them – young people hurrying along the street, heads bent over their cell phones and frantically tapping away at their keyboards, totally oblivious to their surroundings.

Even if you don't have a cell phone, your iPad allows you to do the same thing (apart from the hurrying bit, perhaps!). This is courtesy of its iMessage service that lets you send text, picture, video and audio messages free of charge.

The only limitation is that the service is exclusive to owners of Apple devices, specifically, the iPad, the iPhone and the iPod Touch – no one else can use it. Messages can be sent to cell phone numbers as well as email addresses.

To use the iMessage service:

1. Open the Messages app

2. If this is the first time you've used the iMessaging service, a log-in window will pop up asking you to sign in with your Apple ID. Enter your details and then tap the Sign In button

3. In the window that opens, tap the New Message ✎ button to open a new message window

4. If the person you're sending the message to is in your Contacts list, tap the ⊕ button to open the list

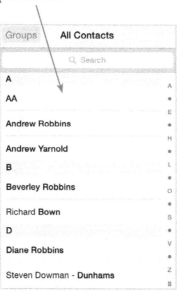

5. Tap on the required contact. If the person is not in your Contacts list, type the phone number or email address in the To: box at the top of the screen

Sending & Receiving Text Messages

Having addressed your message, you are now ready to enter the text and then send it. Tap in the box next to the camera icon and then type your message.

When you have finished typing the message, tap Send at the bottom-right corner of the window. As replies come in, the Messages app icon on the Home screen will show a red badge at the top-right corner indicating the number of messages received. Tap the icon to see what they are.

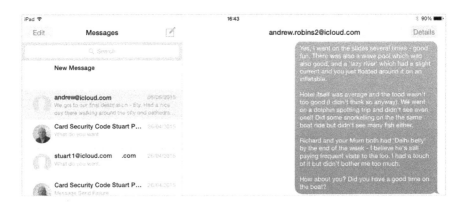

In the message window, you will notice that your messages are highlighted in grey bubbles on the left and replies are highlighted in blue bubbles on the right – this makes it easy to distinguish between them.

To send a reply yourself, tap in the box next to the camera icon as before.

Options include tapping Edit at the top-left, which lets you edit the conversation. While in Edit mode, you can select conversations by tapping on them and then delete them.

Sending Media Messages

The Messages app is not restricted to text – it can also be used to send pictures, video, audio, and your location.

Sending Pictures and Videos

Text messages may have been all the rage at one time but picture and video messages are the in-thing these days.

1. Open the Messages app

2. Tap the New Message icon at the top

3. Tap the camera icon at the left of the text field. This opens a pop-up that gives you two options: 'Photo Library' and 'Take Photo or Video'

4. If you tap 'Photo Library' another window will open showing all the albums in the Photos app – tap one and then scroll through the thumbnails until you find the picture or video you want to send

5. Tap the picture or video and then tap Use at the top-right. This inserts the picture/video into the message. If you want to add some text, you can do so by typing into the text field next to the camera icon. Finally, tap Send

6. Going back to Step 3 and the option to 'Take Photo or Video'. If you select this, the Camera app is opened from where you can elect to take either a picture or a video

    Having done so, you will see 'Retake' at the bottom-left of the picture or video and 'Use Photo' at the bottom-right. If you tap the latter, the picture/video is inserted into your message. Then tap Send. Note that you can insert any number of pictures or videos in a message

Sending Audio Clips

Pictures and videos are all well and good but there is yet another type of media that can be sent with the Messages app. This is audio and not only can it convey more information than the other types of media, it can also add a personal touch that words and images cannot.

1. Open the Messages app

2. Open a new message window

3. Press and hold the microphone icon at the right of the text field. You will now see the following:

4. Speak your message. As you're doing so, you'll see an audio waveform being created. To stop recording, release the icon. To recommence recording, press and hold again. If you want to delete the recording, tap the X. When you are ready to send it, tap the arrow icon at the top

Sending Your Location

'Where are you?' is a common question. The Messages app lets you answer it by sending a map that pinpoints your precise location. Furthermore, if other people in a conversation are also sharing their locations, you will see them in the message thread on a map as well. To do this:

1. Open a conversation and then tap Details at the top-right

2. Tap 'Send My Current Location'

3. Alternatively, you can tap 'Share My Location'. This opens a pop-up that offers three options regarding the length of time that you want your location to be shared for. Just tap the required option

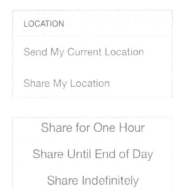

Note that if 'Share My Location' has been selected, your location will be updated automatically if it changes. This is assuming that you have Location Services activated in the iPad's settings.

Video Calls

FaceTime is an iPad feature that lets you make video calls to users of other Apple devices (iPad, iPhone, iPod Touch, and Mac computers). During these video calls, both parties can see each other.

Calls made with FaceTime are absolutely free. However, if you are using a cellular connection, do keep an eye on your data allowance.

Setting Up FaceTime

Before you can make a FaceTime call, you need to set up FaceTime as we explain below:

1. Open the FaceTime app

2. Enter your Apple ID and password

3. Tap Sign In

4. Specify the email address you want other people to use when they call you

Making a FaceTime Call

Initiating a FaceTime video call can be done in the following ways:

1. Open the FaceTime app and enter the name, number or email address of the person you want to contact. Or, if you have recently spoken to the person, their number may be in the list below – select it from there.

   Then tap the FaceTime button – the number will now ring

2. Open the Contacts app and select the required contact. Then tap FaceTime

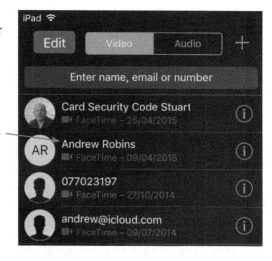

While the call is in progress, you'll see three icons on the screen. Tapping the camera icon at the left switches to the rear camera, thus letting you show the other person what's in front of you.

The red phone icon in the middle lets you end the call, while the microphone icon at the right lets you mute the sound at your end (you will still be able to hear the other person though).

Social Networking

Social media websites such as Facebook, Twitter and Flickr are increasingly being used as a means of keeping in touch with friends and family. In the past, the iPad's support for social networking has not been great but with the Pro, Air 2 and Air models that has changed.

Thanks to the improvements built-in to iOS 9 your iPad has the potential to act as the hub for your social networking activities. It is now possible to link all your social networking sites to the iPad and use the device to upload content, receive alerts from the Notification Center, and view updates in Safari.

1. Tap the Settings app on the Home screen

2. On the left-hand side of the screen, you'll see your social networking options – these include Twitter, Facebook, Flickr and Vimeo

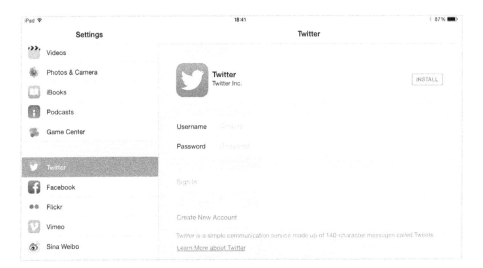

3. Tap the required option to open its settings screen on the right

4. Tap the Install button to download and install the app

5. If you already have an account with the site, log in with your username and password. If not, tap 'Create New Account' to set one up

From this point on, you can upload pictures and videos from your iPad directly from the relevant apps.

For example, open the Photos app, select a picture and then tap the Share button. In the Share menu, you will see the four social networking websites mentioned above. Just tap on one to upload the selected picture to the site.

CHAPTER 8

Organization

In Chapter 8, we see how your iPad can be gainfully employed in helping to organize your life. This is done with the aid of four apps supplied with the device – Contacts, Calendar, Reminders and Notes. Of these, Contacts and the Calendar are perhaps the most useful and will make it easy to stay in touch with the people in your life.

The Reminders and Notes apps help you to remember all the little things that need attention during your day. We also take a look at the Do Not Disturb app and see what can done with it.

Creating & Editing Contacts

Addresses and landline telephone numbers are no longer enough – these days there's also mobile numbers, email addresses and website addresses to be remembered. Step forward the electronic version of the traditional address book – the Contacts app.

Adding Contacts

When you first open it, the Contacts app will be empty. If you're like most people though, it won't be that way for too long.

1. Having opened the app from the Home screen, tap the + sign at the top of the screen – this opens the New Contact window

2. You will see a list of available information fields. Scroll down to see them all

3. The three fields at the top are for the contact's first and last names, plus Company. Tap in each field and then enter the names. If you wish to assign a picture to the contact, tap 'add photo' at the top-left. You will see two options: 'Take Photo' and 'Choose Photo'. The former opens the Camera app allowing you to take a picture, and the latter opens the Photos app from where you can select a picture

4. Next, you'll see 'add phone'. Tapping this will enable you to enter the contact's home phone number. If you tap it again, you'll be able to enter a work phone number. Keep tapping and you will see even more phone number fields

    If you tap a field name, e.g. home, a list of available fields will open as shown on the right. This includes an 'Add Custom Label' option that lets you create your own field

Cancel	Label	Done
home		✓
work		
iPhone		
mobile		
main		
home fax		
work fax		
pager		
other		

5. Below 'add phone' is 'add email'. Available fields here include home, work, iCloud and other. You can also create your own field as described above

6. Moving down the screen, you'll see options for add URL, add address, add birthday, add date, add related name, add social profile, add instant message and add field

    With all these options, tapping the field name opens a list of available fields. The last one, 'add field' enables you to create your own fields and, with it, you can add information of any conceivable type to a contact

Editing Contacts

Having created a list of contacts, you will no doubt want at some point to edit one or more of them. This is very easy to do:

1. Open the Contacts app

2. Tap the contact to be edited

3. Tap Edit at the top-right of the window

4. The original information is now available and can be changed where necessary. When you are finished, tap Done at the top-right – your changes will be saved

Deleting Contacts

Should you wish to delete a contact, open the contact's Edit screen as described above and scroll down to the bottom. Here, you'll see a Delete Contact option in red.

Finding & Using Contacts

Tap the Contacts app – it will open in the following view:

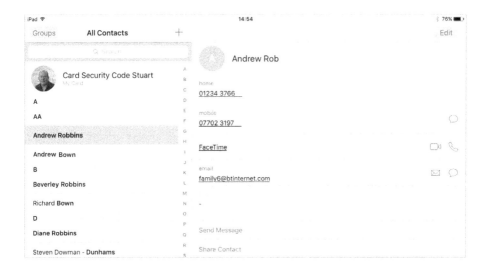

On the left of the screen, you will see an alphabetical list of all the people for whom the app holds information. On the right, the details of the selected contact are displayed.

Finding Contacts

If you have a long list of contacts, you may have to scroll down the screen to find the one you want. You can avoid the need to do this by tapping the relevant blue capital letter at the right of the contacts list – all contacts filed under this letter will now be moved to the top of the list.

Alternatively, you can use the search box, which you will find at the top. As you type in letters, the search box will quickly whittle the list down to the required contact.

Using Contacts

Tap the desired contact and, on the right of the screen, you will see all the information held for that contact. If you have a cellular iPad, just tap a phone number to initiate a call to it; for email, tap any email address to open a pre-addressed message window in the Mail app; and tap any website address to open the site in Safari.

At the far-right, you'll see various icons. The bubble icon next to cell phone numbers opens the Messages app; the camera and phone icons next to FaceTime open FaceTime video and phone links respectively; while the envelope and bubble icons next to email addresses open the Mail and Message apps.

Contacts App Settings

As with most of the apps on your iPad, the Contacts app has a number of settings that can be configured to suit your method of working or requirements. These can be accessed by opening the Settings app and then tapping Mail, Contacts, Calendars. Scroll down to the Contacts Section.

CONTACTS	
Sort Order	Last, First >
Display Order	First, Last >
Short Name	>
My Info	Card Security Code Stuart >
Contacts Found in Mail	⬤

The options are:

Sort Order – this lets you sort your contacts from A to Z by 'First Name, Last Name' or 'Last Name, First Name'.

Display Order – this lets you specify how your contacts names are displayed – 'First Name, Last Name' or 'Last Name, First Name'. Together, these two settings provide four possible combinations for sorting and displaying your contacts.

Short Name – by default, both the Messages and Mail apps show only the first name of a contact in a conversation thread. For those of us that have more than one 'John' in our contacts, for example, this can be the cause of unnecessary confusion. The setting lets you turn Short Names off completely or choose from various options such as 'First Name & Last Initial', 'First Name Only', etc.

My Info – My Info is your personal details and it is used by the iPad's AutoFill feature – see page 94. It tells Siri your name and any relationships you have, and also works with Find my iPhone. To use it, you have to first create a contact for yourself and then select that contact by tapping My Info.

Contacts Found in Mail – this lets the iPad scan your email for contact information like phone numbers and email addresses. By doing so, it is able to suggest auto-complete addresses in Mail. It also enables it to make an educated guess on an incoming call as to who's calling you, if the name and number aren't in your Contacts list yet but are in one of your emails. If you don't like the idea of this, tap the switch to Off.

The Calendar App

People live busy lives these days – they have places to go, people to see. The busier they are, the more things they have to remember and this is where the electronic calendar comes into play.

Provided with your iPad is an extremely useful calendar that will ensure you never again forget a birthday, business appointment, lunch date, or anniversary. The calendar remembers all these dates and times and can also prompt you with reminders just to make sure you don't forget.

On the Home page, tap Calendar:

The app has four views and opens at the view in use when it was last closed down. These are Day, Week, Month and Year, and can be selected at the top of the screen.

- **Day** – in this view, you see the events for the selected day. A timeline and list of events is displayed on the left, and details of the events on the right. A red horizontal line indicates the current time

- **Week** – this view shows all the events in any given week and the time they are scheduled for – you may have to scroll down to see them all

- **Month** – in the Month view, you see all the events in any given month, and the days and times they are scheduled for

- **Year** – this view shows the full calendar year with the current day highlighted in red. No other information is shown. Tap any month to go to the Month view for that month

At the top-right of the screen is a icon. Tap this to open a search box that is very useful with busy calendars. As you type, relevant entries appear in a results list – when you see the one you want, tap to go to it.

At the bottom is a navigation bar that provides three options – Today, Calendars and Inbox. Tapping Today will immediately take you to the current day wherever you are in the calendar; Calendars opens a list of all your calendars (we'll see more on this later); and Inbox shows any calendar invitations you may have received, plus any replies you have made.

With the iPad in Landscape mode and Day view selected, tapping the days of the week at the top of the screen takes you to those days. You can also move between days by flicking left and right at the left of the screen.

In Week view, you can move between weeks by flicking left and right anywhere on the screen.

In the Month and Year views, scroll up and down to move between months and years respectively. Also, while in these two views tapping an event opens a window that displays the details of that event.

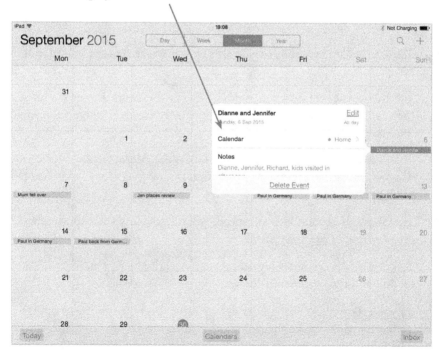

Adding Events to a Calendar

An 'event' is calendar-speak for an entry. To add an event to a calendar, follow these steps:

1. The first thing to do is select the day on which the event is to occur

2. Next, tap the + icon at the top-right of the screen. This opens the New Event window shown on the right

3. Tap in the Title box and type in a suitable name for the event

4. Do the same in the Location box

5. Tap in the Starts box and select a time for your event to begin. Note that you can also set the date here

6. Do the same in the Ends box

7. If the event is a recurring one, tap in the Repeat box and select one of the provided options

8. Again, if the event is recurring, set an end date in the End Repeat box

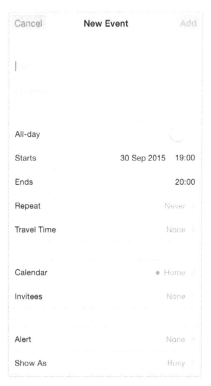

9. The Travel Time section lets you specify the travelling time allocated to the event

10. The Invitees section lets you invite people to the event. Tap in the box and then tap the + icon – this opens your contacts list from where you can add the invited person's email address

11. To ensure you don't forget the event, tap in the Alerts section. This opens a window providing a number of alert options, ranging from 5 minutes to 1 week before

12. The Show As section lets you specify your availability status during an event – options are Busy and Free

13. You can also make notes regarding your calendar by tapping in the Notes section and typing them in the box

Should you ever wish to change the details for an event, go to the event, tap Edit at the top-right, make the changes and then tap Done.

Working With Multiple Calendars

A great feature of calendar apps in general is that they let you create any number of calendars – you are not restricted to just one. This also applies to the iPad's Calendar app – it provides four default calendars – iCloud, Home, Calendar and Work. You also have the option to create more.

Accessing Calendars
To access your calendars, open the Calendar app and tap Calendars on the navigation bar at the bottom of the screen. This opens a window that shows the four calendars provided with the app.

You will notice that each has a different color dot to the left – these are for identification purposes. Any calendars that you create will also be shown here.

Should you wish to, you can edit the calendars (apart from the iCloud calendar) by tapping Edit at the top-left and then tapping the calendar to be edited. You will be able to rename the calendar and change the color of the dot associated with it.

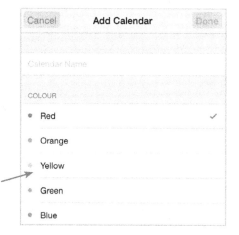

If you scroll down the window, you will see a Delete option that lets you delete the calendar.

Creating Calendars
If you need more calendars than supplied with the app, you can create them easily:

1. Open the Show Calendars screen as described above and tap Edit

2. In the Edit Calendars screen, tap 'Add Calendar...'

3. In the Add Calendar screen, give your calendar a name and select a color for it

4. Tap Done and then Done again

In the Show Calendars window, your new calendar will now be listed.

Viewing Calendars

By default, all calendars are lumped together, i.e. events from all of them appear on the same calendar. For example, if you have a dentists appointment on April 27th on your Home calendar and a business meeting also on April 27th on your Work calendar, when you open the Calendar app and go to April 27th, you will see both events even though they are on different calendars.

This also applies to events on any calendars you create yourself. You can always tell which event belongs to which calendar by the colored dot to the left of the event's name. However, you may only want to see events from a specific calendar, in which case:

1. Open the Calendar app

2. Tap Calendars on the navigation bar at the bottom of the screen

3. The Show Calendars window will open displaying a list of all your calendars

4. You will see each calendar has a checkmark to its left, indicating it has been selected. Deselect the ones whose events you don't want to see by tapping them to remove the checkmark

As you deselect a calendar, its events are removed from all calendars

Default Calendar

When you have a number of calendars, you will need to know which one is in use when you create a new event, i.e. which is the default calendar.

You can set this by opening the Settings app and going to Mail, Contacts, Calendar. On the right, scroll down to the Calendars section. At the bottom of this you will see 'Default Calendar' and, to the right, the current default calendar.

If you want to make a different calendar the default, tap on 'Default Calendar' to open a list of all your calendars – just select the one you want as the default by tapping it.

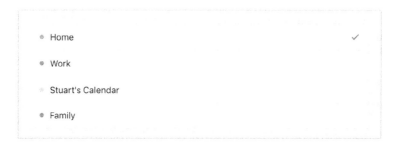

Adding an Alert to an Event

If you're the type of person who tends to forget things, one of the most useful features of electronic calendars may provide the answer. We're talking here about the Calendar app's Alert feature, which will let you know about an upcoming event a set period beforehand.

Setting an Alert
To ensure you don't forget a birthday or whatever:

1. Open the calendar and go to the date that contains the event

2. Tap the event and the event information window opens

3. Tap Edit

4. The Edit Event window opens – tap Alert

5. You will see a number of options: At time of event, 15 minutes before, 1 hour before, 1 day before, etc – select the one you want. Note that if you are setting an alert for an all-day event, the options are slightly different

6. Tap Done

Edit Event	**Alert**
None	
At time of event	
5 minutes before	
15 minutes before	
30 minutes before	
1 hour before	
2 hours before	
1 day before	
2 days before	
1 week before	

Should you feel the need, you can also set a backup alert in case the first one doesn't get your attention.

1. Follow steps 1 to 3 above

2. Tap Second Alert

3. Select the required alert period and tap Done

When the alert activates, the Calendar app will automatically display a reminder of the event on the screen. Just to make sure you get the message, your iPad will also emit a beep.

Finally, the Calendar app provides a useful time-saving feature that lets you set default alert times for different types of event. Open the Settings app and go to Mail, Contacts, Calendars. Tap 'Default Alert Times' and you'll be presented with options for setting alert periods for Birthdays, Events, and All-Day Events.

The Reminders App

The Calendar app is excellent for tracking appointments, meetings, etc. You can also make sure you don't forget the appointment or meeting by adding an alert to it as we have just seen.

But what about the multitude of daily tasks that need to be done at specific times but do not really warrant a calendar entry and alert? Examples include taking the cake out of the oven, watching a program on the TV, calling someone, etc.

The solution is another of your iPad's apps – the Reminders app:

Setting a Reminder

Reminders can be set up in the following way:

1. Open the Reminders app

2. On the left-hand side, you'll see the default lists – tap the Reminders list

3. In the Reminders screen on the right, tap anywhere and type the name of the new reminder

4. Tap the ⓘ button at the far-right of the reminder

5. The Details window opens. Tap the 'Remind me on a day' switch to the On position

6. Tap Alarm – set the required date and time for the reminder

7. If you want the reminder to be a recurring one, tap Repeat and select the required option: Every Day, Every Week, Every Month, etc

8. You can specify a priority level for the reminder by tapping the required level – !, !!, or !!! – the latter is the highest priority level

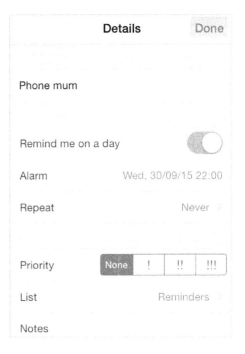

9. If you want to include a note regarding the reminder, tap Notes and type in your text

10. Finally, tap Done at the top-right of the window

Hiding & Deleting Reminders

When you have finished with a reminder, there are two ways to get rid of it – hide it or delete it.

Hiding Reminders
Open the list containing the reminder to be hidden. To the left of the reminder, you will see a round radio button.

Tap the button and a colored dot will appear inside it, which indicates the reminder has been selected. Now close the list. The next time you open it, the reminder will be gone.

However, this doesn't mean the reminder has been deleted. If you wish to see it again for some reason or to reactivate it, tap 'Show Completed' at the bottom of the list it was in. A list will be displayed showing all the reminders you have created in that list. To reactivate one, tap the radio button to remove the colored dot.

Deleting Reminders
Open the list containing the reminder to be deleted. Place your finger to the right of the reminder and drag it to the left. This will reveal a More button and a Delete button, as shown below:

Tap the Delete button to remove the reminder permanently. The More button opens the reminder's Details window from where you can edit it if you so wish.

Working With Lists

The Reminders app provides you with two default reminder lists – Reminders and Scheduled. You will see them on the left of the screen.

Creating Lists

You may find, though, that these are not enough. You might, for example, need some extra lists to keep your home and work reminders separate. Whatever the reason, you can create your own lists as we see below:

1. Open the Reminders app

2. At the bottom-left of the screen, tap Add List

3. Type the name for your list

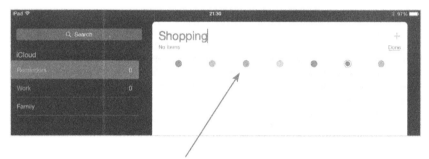

4. Tap to select an identifying color and then tap Done

Your new list will now be available on the left of the screen.

Moving and Deleting Lists

You can easily rearrange the order of your lists:

1. At the bottom-right of the Lists section, tap Edit

2. You'll see a ≡ icon appear to the right of each list. Place your finger on it and move it up or down to move the list. Then tap Done

To delete a list, tap the red icon at the left of the list. A Delete button slides into view at the right. Tap it and then tap Delete in the confirmation window.

The Notes App

The Notes app is a standard iPad application that allows you to quickly jot down notes as they come to mind. While there are many apps of this type available in the App Store, some offering more features, the Notes app is straightforward and easy to use.

Creating Notes

Creating a note with the Notes app is extremely simple. To do it:

1. Open the app by tapping Notes on the Home screen

2. At the top-right of the screen, tap the New Note icon

3. A new note window opens and the keyboard slides into view allowing you to type your note

4. When you are finished, the app automatically saves the note – you don't have to tap a Save button

5. At the left is a list of all your notes together with the time they were created (assuming it was done within the last 24 hours). The time-stamp will change to a date-stamp if the note goes back further than a day

Editing Notes

To edit a note, tap its name on the left to open it in the editing window on the right. Tap anywhere in the window and the keyboard will open allowing you to make your changes to the note.

Formatting Notes

Quite apart from changing the note's text, you can also change the way it is formatted. It is also possible to insert pictures in your notes.

Lets take a look at the former first:

1. Press and hold on the text to be formatted. Lift your finger when the magnifying glass appears

2. On the menu bar, tap Select. Then select the required text

3. The menu bar will now be showing a B*I*U option – tap it and select from Bold, Italics and Underline

To insert a picture, do the following:

1. Move the cursor to the required insertion point

2. At the top-right of the keyboard, you will see a camera button

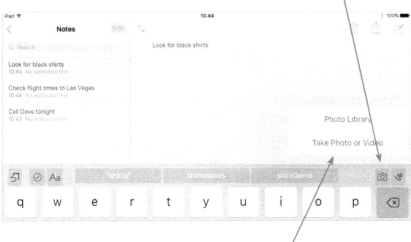

3. Tap the camera button to reveal 'Photo Library' and 'Take Photo or Video' options. The former takes you to the Photos app from where you can select a picture, and the latter opens the camera app so you can take a picture

Deleting Notes

Notes that you no longer want can be deleted in two ways. The simplest is to open the note and then tap the Trash icon at the top-right. Then tap Delete Note in the confirmation window.

Alternatively, tap the Edit button at the top-right of the notes list. A selection box will open at the left of each note. Check the ones you want to delete and then tap Delete at the bottom-right.

Do Not Disturb

While the iPad may be an excellent device for communication purposes and getting audio alerts and reminders, etc, there will inevitably be times when you simply do not want to hear from it. The solution is to activate a feature called, not surprisingly, Do Not Disturb. Use it as follows:

1. Open the Settings app

2. Tap the Do Not Disturb tab on the left-hand side of the screen

3. If you want to silence the iPad until further notice, tap the Manual option

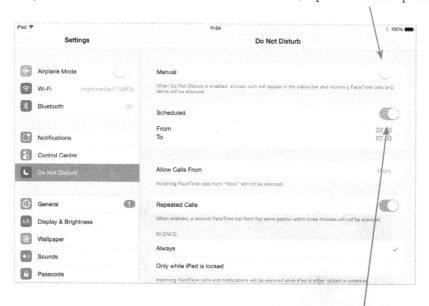

4. If you just want to silence it for a certain period, tap the Scheduled switch to On. This opens From and To time options that let you specify precisely the period in which you do not want to be disturbed

5. There may, however, be people who you don't want to silence. In this case, tap 'Allow Calls From' and select them from the available options

A potential problem with activating the Do Not Disturb feature is that it will then be impossible to contact you with the iPad in an emergency. You can get round this by tapping Repeated Calls to On; now your iPad will respond to successive FaceTime calls separated by less than three minutes.

Using Maps

The Maps feature provided with your iPad is an extremely handy application that can be used for a number of purposes. These include getting directions to a particular place, getting information about a place, finding out your current location, getting live traffic information, and more.

Getting Directions

Your iPad always knows where it is – cellular models have a built-in GPS receiver and Wi-Fi models use nearby Wi-Fi hotspots to get an approximate fix. As a result, it can give you precise directions to and from any location. You can use these to guide you when walking or driving.

1. Tap the Maps app – it opens showing the iPad's current location

2. Tap Directions at the top-left

3. In the pop-up window, enter the start location in the Start: box and the destination in the End: box.

4. Tap Route at the top-right, or on the keyboard, and the map view will now zoom out and show you two or three of the best routes along with the travelling time involved. Tap anywhere on the route you want to use

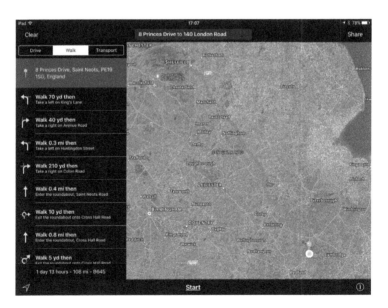

5. At the top, tap Drive or Walk. Then tap Start at the bottom

As you travel, you will be given turn-by-turn directions, such as 'in 50 yards, turn into Kings Road'. You can see your position on the route, distance and time remaining, a text list of all turns, and more.

Live Traffic Information
The Maps app may say a certain route will take, say, 30 minutes but out there in the real world traffic conditions will probably be dictating something completely different.

To find out, tap the Information button at the bottom-right of the screen. In the information window, tap Show Traffic.

If there are any known hold-ups in the selected route, a dashed red line will be displayed on the affected section of the route. Also, labelled icons on the map will show the location of construction sites, roadworks, etc.

Get Information About a Place
To bone-up on a particular place, open the Maps app and type the place's name or address in the search box at the top. Assuming the app recognizes the place, it will drop a green pin on its location on the map.

Tap on the pin to open the pop-up window shown on the right. Now tap on the window to open the Information window where you will see phone numbers, address, website address, pictures, and reviews (taken from Yelp).

Find Out Your Current Location
When you're out-and-about in an unfamiliar town, perhaps on holiday, it's always good to know where you are. If your iPad is to hand, the Maps app will ensure that you always do.

Open the app and then tap the Tracking button at the bottom-left of the screen. The map will zoom in and indicate your precise location with a blue dot. Tap the dot for more information.

Refreshments
Once you've established where you are, it may be nice to chill-out with a beer or get something to eat. Once again, your iPad can help. If it's food you want, type restaurant in the search box – the Maps app will immediately drop red pins on all the restaurants it knows about.

Tap on each pin to get directions, the distance, the telephone number, the address, the opening hours, and reviews (taken from Tripadvisor).

Useful Organization Apps

The organization apps supplied with the iPad are not the best examples of their type. You will find better ones, not to mention a much greater selection, in the App Store. Some well known apps are:

Evernote
Used by millions of people all over the world, Evernote is probably the most popular of all the note-taking apps. It offers a text editor, photo upload tool, voice recording, plus some excellent tools that make it a snap to organize, find, and edit your notes.

Also, all your notes are saved in the Cloud – this means they can be accessed from any device and from any location as long as an Internet connection is available.

OneNote
From the maker of the Windows operating system, Microsoft, OneNote is another well regarded note-taking app. As with Evernote, all the notes you create are saved in the Cloud and can thus be accessed on other devices.

Features include the ability to make annotations, tagging, password protection, and Touch ID support. It is also completely free, unlike Evernote where it is necessary to pay for a premium account in order to access all its features.

Dropbox
Dropbox is an online file storage service that lets you save pictures, videos and documents in the Cloud from your iPad and then access them on other devices. Content in your Dropbox can be shared with others and is effectively backed up should anything happen to your iPad.

Alarm Clock HD
To make sure you're always on time and don't forget to do things, the Alarm Clock HD app is a worthy addition to your iPad. You can configure it to use your own pictures for the background and your own music for the sound. There are also preset sounds you can choose from.

Errands To-Do List
This is a task manager that can organize your tasks into folders for easy viewing, create checklists, and set alerts for tasks. You can create new tasks from completed ones – a big time-saver given that many tasks are repetitive. Another useful feature lets you turn a list into a checklist.

PocketLife Calendar
A very handy little calendar app with which to organize your life. Features include cloud synchronization with Google, Outlook, iCal, Yahoo and iCloud, reminders, multiple calendars, recurring events, support for AirDrop and AirPrint, password protection, and more. It is also highly customizable.

CHAPTER 9

Entertainment

In Chapter 9, we see how you can use your iPad as an entertainment center. Not only can you take pictures and home videos with it, you can also edit and organize them into albums to show to other people. One of the iPad's best features though, is its ability to play video and music. Movies, TV programs and music tracks can be bought and downloaded from the iTunes Store and then played wherever you happen to be – a plane, a train, the bus – it doesn't matter.

Taking Pictures

To take a picture with the iPad, tap the Camera app on the Home screen. Alternatively, open the Control Center by swiping upwards from the bottom edge of the screen and then tap the camera icon to open the app.

When the app is open, you'll see the camera controls at the right of the screen.

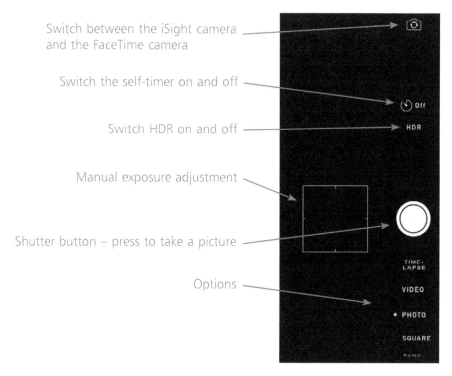

Switch between the iSight camera and the FaceTime camera

Switch the self-timer on and off

Switch HDR on and off

Manual exposure adjustment

Shutter button – press to take a picture

Options

TIME-LAPSE

VIDEO

• PHOTO

SQUARE

PANO

Lets look at these controls in more detail to see what they do:

- The camera button at the top lets you choose either the iSight camera or the FaceTime camera – nothing else

- The self-timer enables you to set a 3 or 10 second delay when taking pictures – this is great for when you want to be in the picture yourself. Compose your shot, then tap the shutter button – a numbered countdown will begin on the screen to indicate that the timer is counting down

- HDR stands for High Dynamic Range image and the feature combines two pictures, each shot at a different exposure. The best parts of these images are put together into one image that brings out details in both the shadows and the highlights – information that would normally be lost in a single exposure

- The manual exposure adjustment enables you to set the exposure yourself. To do it, tap on the screen – this will open a yellow square with a sun icon to the right of it. If you think the exposure could do with adjusting, i.e. the image is either too bright or to dark, swipe your finger up to brighten it or down to darken it. Then take the picture

- Tap the shutter button to take a picture

- The Options section lets you do the following:

  1. The time-lapse feature enables you to shoot a video and then speed up the replay so that everything appears to move much more quickly. For example, a 40 minute clip will take about 20 seconds to play back

  2. Select Video to switch the camera to Video mode

  3. Select Photo to switch the camera to Photo mode

  4. Select Square if you want to take a picture that is square – these are currently in vogue on social media websites, and are used in identification documents such as passports

  5. Short for Panorama, PANO mode lets you capture panoramas – much larger pictures that would otherwise be possible – with the iSight camera. It does this by taking a video-like stream of successive frames and then stitching them together to create a single panoramic picture

If you have a Pro, Air 2, or Mini 4 iPad, the Camera app also provides Burst mode. To use this, you must select either Photo or Square. Then, instead of tapping to take individual pictures, hold the shutter button down to take a rapid series of pictures (10 every second).

Burst mode is ideal for situations where you don't want to risk not getting a good picture. Having taken a series of pictures in this way, you can then examine them individually in the Camera Roll, select the ones you want, and delete those that are not up to scratch.

Viewing Pictures

Having taken some pictures, you will now want to view the results of your photographic endeavours. To do so, tap the Photos app on the Home screen.

The Photos app
The Photos app keeps all the pictures and videos you shoot together in one place. This makes it easier to find them later when you want to view, edit, or share them with someone.

The app automatically sorts your pictures and videos into three 'smart groups', based on time and location. The smallest group is Moments, the next is Collections, and the largest is Years. These enable you to instantly see the date each picture was taken, group them by month, and see the exact location where they were taken on a map.

Navigating Between Smart Groups
Moving between groups can be confusing initially. To do it, tap the back button at the top-left of the screen to move to a larger group. The button will be labelled with the name of the group you'll be moving to – Collections in the example below:

When you want to move the other way, i.e. to a smaller group, simply tap anywhere on the screen.

Viewing Picture and Video Locations on a Map
Not only do the Moments, Collections, and Years smart groups tell you where your pictures and videos were taken, they can also pinpoint those locations on a map.

To do it, simply tap on the name of the location. A map will open showing a thumbnail of the picture and its precise location on the map.

Viewing Pictures

To view a picture, you need to be in the Moments view. If you happen to be in the Years view, tap anywhere on the screen to go to Collections. Find the thumbnail of your picture and tap it – you will now see a larger view of it in Moments. Tap this and it will open in a full-screen view.

While in the Moments and Collections views, you will notice that picture thumbnails are arranged by date taken and, if taken away from your home, by the location they were taken at.

In the Years view, they are grouped by year and location (this includes all the various locations).

Manipulating Pictures

Unlike some picture-viewing devices, the iPad provides you with a number of ways to view your images. These include:

- Scrolling or flicking – if the iPad is in Landscape mode, you can move from one picture to the next, or to the previous one, by flicking left and right

- Rotating – when you view a portrait shot in Landscape mode, there will be a blank area on either side of the picture. Rotating the iPad into Portrait mode will display the picture in full-screen view

- Flipping – if you wish to show a picture to someone, rather than turning the iPad round, simply flip it so that what was the top is now the bottom. The picture will also be flipped so it is the right way up

- Zooming – if you want a close-up of a picture, you can zoom into it. This can be done in two ways:

  1. Double-tap on the part of the picture you want a close-up of – the picture will double in size. Double-tap again to return it to its normal size

  2. Place two fingers on the picture and spread them to zoom in. Close them to zoom back out

- Panning – when you are zoomed in on a picture, you may not be able to see all of it on the screen. If so, place your finger on the screen and drag it about, or pan, to view all the picture

- Scrubbing – see the next page

Finding Pictures Quickly

In previous versions of iOS, finding a particular picture could be somewhat difficult, particularly if it was in an album containing lots of others.

iOS 9 comes to the rescue by adding a 'scrubber' bar at the bottom of your albums. To use it:

1. Open the Photos app and the open the required album

2. Tap on any picture within the album

3. The picture will open full-screen

4. At the bottom of the screen, you will see a scrubber bar that shows thumbnails of all the pictures in the album

5. You can open pictures by tapping the thumbnails on the scrubber bar. However, its main use is to quickly find the picture you are looking for. To do this, simply place a finger on the bar and move it left and right. As you do so, the pictures will flash past sequentially in full-screen view. When you get to the one you want, take your finger off the bar

The scrubber bar makes it a breeze to navigate photo albums that contain a lot of pictures.

Creating Photo Albums

It is very common for people to organize their pictures into photo albums so it is easy to find them later on. On the iPad, this is another of the functions provided by the Photos app:

1. Open the Photos app

2. At the bottom of the screen, tap Albums

3. At the top-left of the screen, tap the + icon

4. In the New Album window that opens, type a name for the album and then tap Save. In the example below, we have created an album in which to place holiday snaps taken in Las Vegas

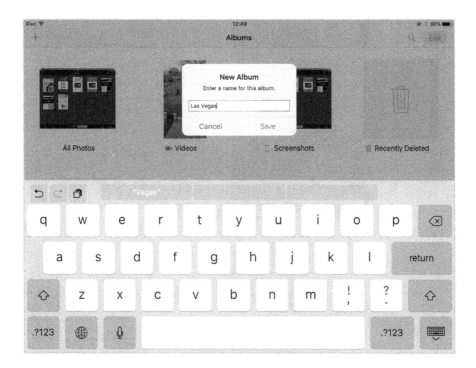

5. The Photos app will now switch to the Moments view

6. Using the Select buttons on the right of the screen, select the pictures to be placed in the new album

7. Tap Done

8. The Photos app now switches to the Album view where you will see your new album. Open the album and the pictures you selected in Step 6 will be there

Uploading Pictures to the iPad

While the iPad's iSight camera takes pictures of decent enough quality, those taken by a digital camera are definitely of a higher standard. However, where the iPad does have the advantage is its large screen, which is much better at displaying pictures than the small screen offered by the typical digital camera.

For this reason, many people use a digital camera to take their pictures and then upload them to the iPad for showing to friends and family. There are two ways this can be done:

Uploading from a Computer to the iPad
The first is to upload the pictures from a computer to the iPad. To do this, you will need to use iTunes:

1. Connect the iPad to the computer

2. Start iTunes

3. In iTunes, click the iPad button

4. Click Photos on the sidebar at the left

5. In the window that opens, check the 'Sync Photos' checkbox

6. Click 'Copy photos from', select 'Choose folder', and then browse to the folder that contains the required pictures

7. When you have found the folder, click 'Select Folder' at the bottom and then click Apply at the bottom-right of the iTune's screen – the pictures in the folder will be now be uploaded to the iPad

8. When the upload is complete, go to the iPad and open the Photos app

9. Tap Albums at the bottom of the screen to show the Album view. You will see a new folder containing the uploaded pictures

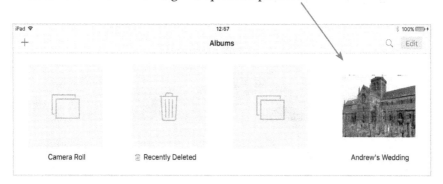

At this point, you may think the job is done – the pictures are on the iPad, what else is there to do? However, if you leave the newly uploaded pictures where they are, the next time you use this method to upload pictures, they will be overwritten by the new ones. So your final task is to move them to a different folder as described on the next page.

Uploading from a Camera to the iPad
The second way to upload pictures to your iPad is to transfer them directly from a digital camera. This requires the use of a specially designed adaptor. Apple provides two types:

● **Lightening to USB Camera Adaptor** – the camera adaptor has a USB interface that plugs into the dock connector port on your iPad. Then you attach your digital camera with a USB cable

● **Lightening to SD Card Camera Reader** – connect the SD card reader to your iPad, then insert your camera's SD card into the slot

Whichever adaptor you use, after the connection is made, your iPad automatically opens the Photos app. This lets you choose which pictures to import, prior to organizing into albums.

Note that both adaptors are supplied with Apple's Camera Connection Kit.

Moving Pictures

Should you ever wish to move a picture from an existing location to a new one, follow this procedure:

1. Open the Photos app in either the Moments or Albums view. If you are in the former, tap Select at the top-right of the screen. If you are in the latter, open the album containing the pictures to be moved and then tap Select at the top-right of the screen

2. In the Select Items screen, locate the desired pictures and tap them once. They will fade slightly and a blue checkmark will appear at the bottom-right of each one indicating they have been selected

3. Tap Add To at the top-left and the 'Add to Album' screen will open as shown below. This contains a newly created album for you to use. Alternatively, you can select an existing album

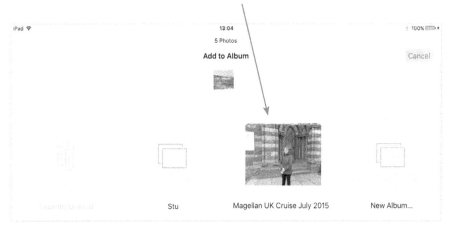

4. Tap 'New Album...', type a name in the Name box and then tap Save. Or, tap an existing album. In either case, the pictures will be moved to the specified album

Deleting Pictures

On the face of it a simple task, deleting a picture is somewhat complicated by the fact that your iPad differentiates between two types of picture:

- Pictures created directly on the iPad. These include those taken with the cameras, copied from an email, the Internet, or some other source

- Pictures copied from a computer and uploaded to the iPad via iTunes

To delete pictures created directly on the iPad:

1. Open the Photos app

2. Locate the picture to be deleted

3. Open the picture by tapping on it. At the top-right of the screen you will see a Trash icon. Tap it then tap Delete Photo

However, if you don't see the Trash icon, it means the picture is a copy uploaded via iTunes and so cannot be deleted with the Photos app. In this case, you need to use a different method:

1. Go to the folder on the computer that contains the original picture and remove it from the folder

2. Connect your iPad to the computer and start iTunes

3. Click the iPad button at the top-left of the screen and then click Photos on the left-hand side

4. In the new window, check the 'Sync Photos' checkbox

5. In the 'Copy photos from' dropdown menu, browse to and select the folder from which you have removed the unwanted picture

6. At the bottom-right of the screen, click the Sync button

iTunes will now synchronize the picture folder on the computer with the Photo app on the iPad. Any pictures on the iPad that are not in the folder will be removed from the iPad. It's somewhat convoluted but does work.

Editing Pictures

Your iPad not only lets you take pictures, it lets you edit them. The editing tools it provides are:

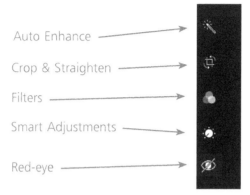

Auto Enhance

Crop & Straighten

Filters

Smart Adjustments

Red-eye

To access the editing tools:

1. Open the Photos app and then tap the picture to be edited

2. At the top-right of the picture, tap Edit

3. You will now see the five editing tools shown above appear on the screen

Lets see what you can do with them:

Auto Enhance
Auto Enhance is basically an all-in-one control. It automatically improves a picture's brightness, color saturation, and other elements.

Crop & Straighten
This tools allows you to do several things:

First, it allows you to straighten a picture that has been taken at an angle. At the left of the picture, you will see a small section of compass. Place your finger on this and move it up and down to adjust the angle.

Second, you can remove parts of a picture that you don't want – this is known as cropping. You do it by specifying a rectangular part of a picture that you want to keep – the rest is discarded.

Cropping can be done manually by dragging the sides of the picture in and out. Alternatively, you can choose from a range of pre-determined crop sizes (shown on the right) by tapping the icon at the bottom-left of the screen.

Original

Square

3:2

5:3

4:3

5:4

7:5

16:9

Filters

The Filter tool provides a range of eight built-in filters. These let you make various changes to the look of your pictures.

Smart Adjustments

The Smart Adjustments tool is three tools in one – Light, Color and B&W.

Selecting each tool opens a 'smart slider', which previews the picture with a range of values. Just drag the slider up and down to alter the picture. The tools intelligently adjust values like saturation, exposure, brightness, and contrast as you move the slider. For more precision, you can also adjust each value individually.

To access these controls, tap the icon on the right side of the list (or bottom depending on the iPad's orientation), then select the value you want to change. For example, for the Light control, you will see the controls shown on the right.

Red-eye

No matter how careful you are, red-eye will occasionally be present in one of your pictures. The last of the Photo app's editing tools is designed to deal with this issue. Simply tap each eye afflicted with red-eye and then tap Done.

Note: You won't see the red-eye correction tool unless you are trying to edit a photo that actually has a red-eye issue. This is because iOS auto-detects red-eye and only shows the tool when it is present.

Printing Pictures & Documents

Whatever type of document you want to print from your iPad, be it an email, picture, or web page, the procedure is the same. However, you will need a printer with Apple's wireless AirPrint technology built-in. If your printer doesn't have it, then you will not be able to print anything from your iPad.

Assuming you have an AirPrint-enabled printer:

1. Open the app containing the document or picture to be printed

2. Look for the Options menu in the app. For example, in the Mail app tap the ⤺ button. In the Photos app and Safari tap the ⬆ button

3. When you have the Options menu open, tap Print

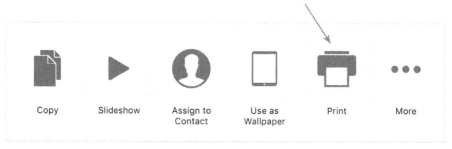

4. If this is the first time you have used the iPad to print something, you will have to associate a printer with it. In the Printer Options screen, tap 'Select Printer >'. The iPad will then look for any wireless printers in the vicinity and display a list of those it has found

5. Tap your AirPrint printer. The iPad will add it to the Printer Options dialogue, and activate the Print button at the bottom

6. In the Copy field, tap the + sign to specify the number of copies to be printed

7. Depending on the printer being used, you may see other options. Configure these as necessary

Cancel	**Printer Options**	
Printer		Select Printer >
Range		All Pages >
1 Copy		— +

8. Tap Print. The iPad sends the document across your wireless network to the printer where it is printed

If you have any problems, check your iPad and printer are both connected to the same Wi-Fi network and that they are within range.

Sharing Pictures

The iPad is the ideal device for sharing your snaps with people around you. How about those who are further afield though? Actually, there are several ways you can do it. These include:

- Email

- Messages

- Photo sharing sites such as Flickr and iCloud Photo Sharing

- Social media sites such as Twitter and Facebook

All the above methods can be used by carrying out the procedure explained below:

1. Open the Photos app and select the picture you want to send

2. Tap the Options ⬆ button at the top-right of the screen

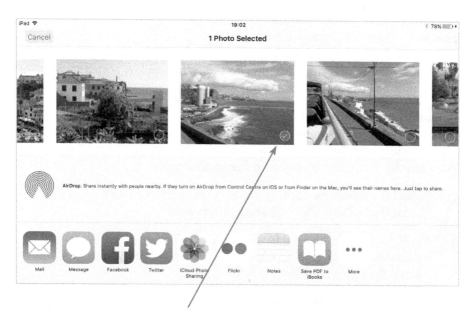

3. At the top, you will see the selected picture – by scrolling left and right, you can select other pictures in the album. Below the pictures are the various sharing options open to you. These are:

Message & Mail

Having selected your pictures, you can text them with the Message app by tapping Message – a New Message window will open. Choose the person you want to share the picture with by tapping the ⊕ icon.

This opens your contacts list from where you can select the recipient. Then tap Send at the bottom-right.

To share a picture by email, tap Mail and follow the same procedure as for Message. Note that you have to tap in the To: field to reveal the ⊕ icon.

Twitter & Facebook
To share pictures via Twitter and Facebook, you first need to set up Twitter and Facebook accounts on your iPad and then sign in to them.

Then (using Facebook as an example), tap Facebook in the Photos app's sharing options. The picture will be added to the Facebook window.

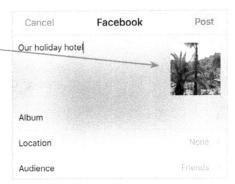

Type in your message (if there is one). Then tap in the Album field to choose which album to post it to, tap Location to specify where you are posting the picture from and, finally, tap Audience to select who can see the picture. Tap Post at the top-right and the picture will be posted to your Facebook timeline.

iCloud Photo Sharing/Flickr
Photo sharing websites allow you to post pictures to a website. You then send the web address of the pictures to whoever you want to share them with. The procedure for doing this with iCloud Photo Sharing is:

1. Enable the feature by opening the Settings app and going to iCloud > Photos. Tap iCloud Photo Sharing to turn it on

2. Tap iCloud Photo Sharing in the Photos app's sharing options. In the window that opens, tap the + button at the top-left, enter a name for the shared album and tap Next.

    In the To: field, enter the email address of the person you want to share with. Alternatively, tap the ⊕ button to open the All Contacts list and select it from there

3. Tap the Create button. The person you want to share with will be now sent an email that contains a link to the web page on which the picture is displayed

4. To share pictures via Flickr, follow the steps above but at Step 2, tap Flickr instead of iCloud Photo Sharing

Recording Home Videos

Although it's not the ideal device with which to record video due to its somewhat awkward dimensions, the iPad will do when nothing better is to hand. To record a video:

1. Open the Camera app

2. Slide the mode switch on the right from Photo to Video – the Shutter/Record button turns from white to red

3. Tap the camera icon at the top to select the camera you want to use – iSight or FaceTime

4. Tap the screen to automatically adjust the focus. If you need to adjust the brightness as well, drag the yellow slider up or down to do so

5. Tap the Record button to start the recording. A timer on the right of the screen will show the length of the recording

6. To stop recording, tap the Record button again

A new feature in iOS 9 allows you to record video at two different resolutions. This can be set as follows:

1. Open the Settings app

2. On the left-hand side, tap Photos & Camera

3. In the Camera section, tap Record Video

4. In the Record Video screen, choose either 720 HD at 30 fps or 1080 HD at 30 fps (the latter provides the highest recording quality)

Locating Your Videos

As with pictures, all videos recorded with the iPad are stored in the Photos app. So when you want to find these videos, this is where you need to go; not the Videos app as you might expect.

1. Open the Photos app and tap Albums at the bottom of the screen

2. You will see an album named Videos

3. Open the Videos album and you will see all the videos you have recorded with the iPad

4. You can also view your videos in the Camera Roll. In this view though, they will be mixed up with your pictures. To differentiate between the two, videos will have a camera icon at the bottom-left and the recording time at the bottom-right of the thumbnail

However, videos, movies and TV programs that have been uploaded from a computer or the iTunes Store *are* stored in the Videos app.

Playing Videos

Playing back your videos is just as simple as viewing your pictures. Do it as follows:

1. Locate the video as described on the previous page and tap to open it

2. Tap the Play icon in the middle of the screen to begin playback

At the bottom of the screen, you'll see a timeline – this shows all the individual frames in the video. If you don't see it, just tap once on the screen. By dragging the timeline left and right, you can quickly move about in the video.

To pause/stop playback, tap on the screen to open the Status bar at the top. At the far-right of the bar, you'll see a blue Pause button – tap it to stop the video. The button now changes to a Play button – tap it to recommence playback.

Also on the Status bar is a heart-shaped Favorites button. Tap this and your video will be saved in a Favorites album in the Photos app. To 'unfavorite' the video, tap the Favorites button again. Next to the Favorites button is an Options button that, amongst other things, lets you share the video via email and post it on social media sites such as YouTube. Next to the Options button is the Trash button that lets you delete the video.

While the video is playing, you can zoom in and out at any time by pinching and stretching two fingers.

Editing Video

A common problem with recording video is that you end up with stuff you don't really want or need. With this in mind, the Photos app provides you with a way of ditching unwanted footage.

On the previous page, we showed how to use the timeline to quickly and easily move about in videos. Well, the timeline has another function – it can also be used as a Trim tool:

1. Open the Photos app and locate the video to be edited

2. Tap on the video to open it. You will now see the timeline below it

3. On the Status bar at the top, tap the Edit button

4. At the beginning and end of the timeline, you'll notice small white arrows

5. Tap and hold either of the arrows and then drag it slightly to the left or right. The entire timeline will now be highlighted in yellow

6. Next, drag the arrow at the left across to the right thus setting the start point of the video. Then drag the arrow at the right across to the left to set the end point of the video

7. The selected frames in the timeline will now be highlighted in yellow

8. Tap Done at the bottom-right of the screen. Then select 'Trim Original' or 'Save as New Clip'

9. The frames not selected are removed from the video, which is then saved in the Photos app

Downloading Movies From the iTunes Store

1. On the iPad's Home screen, tap the iTunes Store app

2. When the Store opens, tap either Movies or TV Programs on the toolbar at the bottom of the screen

3. Find a movie to import. If you know which one you want, use the search box at the top-right to go straight to it. Otherwise, scroll left and right and up and down to see what's available

4. When you have made your choice, tap on the image to see the movie's details. This gives you a summary of the plot, the cast, and info such as the producing studio, date of release, running time, etc

5. Other options include Reviews, which lets you know how others have rated the movie, and Related, which gives you a list of similar movies

6. At the right of the screen, you will see HD and SD buttons. If you want the movie in high-definition, tap HD – SD will give you standard-definition quality. Note that the movie will cost less in SD

7. When you are ready to buy, tap the Buy button.
For a lower charge you can opt to rent by tapping the Rent button

After payment has been taken, the movie is downloaded to your iPad where you will find it in the Videos app.

Uploading Music to the iPad

Uploading From a Computer

One of the first things many iPad users want to do is get their computer-based music collection on to the device. To do this, it is necessary to first place the required music in the iTunes music library:

1. On the computer, open iTunes

2. At the top-left, click File and then click 'Add Folder to Library'

3. Browse to the folder that contains your music collection

4. Select the folder and then click Select Folder at the bottom

Your music collection will now be added to the iTunes music library. The next stage is to transfer it to the iPad:

1. Connect the iPad to the computer and open iTunes

2. In iTunes, click the iPad button under the menu bar at the top-left

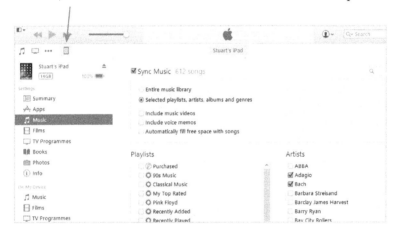

3. In the Settings section on the sidebar, click Music

4. On the right-hand side of the screen, check the Sync Music checkbox

5. You now have a choice to make: transfer your entire music collection or just part of it. If it's the former, select 'Entire Music Library' and if it's the latter, select 'Selected playlists, artists, albums and genres'

6. Beneath these two options, you'll see further options to 'Include Music Videos' and 'Include Voice Memos', both of which are self-explanatory. If you select the 'Automatically fill free space with songs' option, this will fill any remaining space on the iPad with a selection of similar music from the library

7. If you've elected to transfer the entire collection, all you have to do now is click the Sync button at the bottom-right of the screen

8. If you want to transfer just some of the tracks in the collection, however, go to the Artists section on the right of the screen and select the ones you want. Having done so, then click the Sync button

Downloading from the iTunes Store

The easiest way to get music on the iPad is to download it directly to the device from the iTunes Store. Just tap on the iTunes Store app and then when it opens, tap Music on the menu bar at the bottom of the screen.

Browsing the store, and buying and downloading music, is much the same procedure as with buying apps in the App Store so we won't repeat it.

Downloading Via iCloud

This method only applies to music purchased from the iTunes Store. As we saw above, the easiest way to get music on to the iPad is to open the Store on the device and simply download any purchases directly to it.

However, there may be occasions when your iPad is not to hand. In these situations, you can use another iOS device – a Mac, iPhone, or iPod Touch – to buy the music and then have it sent automatically to your iPad. This is known as automatic downloading.

To set it up:

1. Tap the Settings app on the Home screen

2. Tap iTunes & App Store

3. In the Automatic Downloads section, tap the Music switch to the On position

From now on, every time you purchase music from the iTunes Store with any iOS device, it is sent automatically to your iCloud account, and then from there onwards to all your other devices, including the iPad.

Playing Music

Having got some tracks on to your iPad, you will now want to play them. On the Home screen, tap the Music app. When it opens, at the bottom of the screen, you will see an Options toolbar showing a number of icons – tap the one at the far-left – My Music.

This opens a screen similar to the one shown below:

At the top of the screen, in the middle, you will see a button (Artists in the example above). Tap it to reveal a list that provides various options for viewing your music collection.

Having found a track you want to play, tap to open it. You will now see a mini–player at the bottom-left of the screen just above the Options toolbar.

This provides four controls – Previous track, Play, Pause, and Next track. At the top-right is a three-bar icon – tap this to see the Up Next list that shows you the tracks waiting to be played. You can re-order the tracks by placing your finger on the icon at the right of each track and moving them up and down the list.

cont'd

If you want to access the full music player, tap the track information in the middle, or touch and hold the mini-player and drag it up – the full player will slide into view and fill the screen as shown below:

At the bottom of the player are some extra music controls not provided with the mini-player. At the left are Shuffle, which lets you randomly rearrange the order in which tracks are played; and Repeat, which lets you either repeat the song or the artist. In the middle is the volume control and at the right are options that let you share the track or artist via email, messaging and social media; and add the track to a playlist.

You can also play your music from the Control Center. Swipe upwards from the bottom of any screen and the Control Center will slide into view.

The music controls are on the left and will let you play, pause and stop the last track opened in the Music app. You can also adjust the volume and go to the next or previous track using the Previous and Next buttons.

Apple Music

Apple Music is a new service from Apple that enables you to access the entire Apple iTunes library on your iPad. Music can be downloaded to the iPad for offline listening or streamed over the Internet. The service is subscription-based and, at the time of writing, is priced at $9.99 monthly. However, Apple is offering a free three-month trial – if this is something that is of interest to you, get going as we describe below:

Signing Up For Apple Music

To sign up for Apple Music:

1. Open the Music app

2. Tap the For You button on the toolbar at the bottom of the screen

3. Tap the 'Start 3 Month Free Trial' button

4. You are offered the choice of an Individual or Family membership plan – select one

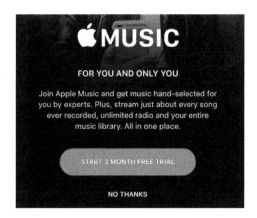

5. Enter your Apple ID password and then tap the OK button

Assuming the password checks out, you are now ready to go. Three months down the line, your free trial will come to an end. You may, at this point, decide that the Apple Music service is worth the cost of the subscription fee. If so, proceed as follows:

1. Open the Settings app

2. Tap 'iTunes & App Store' at the left

3. On the right, at the top, tap your Apple ID (which is in blue text)

4. Tap View Apple ID

5. In the pop-up box, enter your password and tap OK

6. Your account screen will open. In the Subscriptions section, tap Manage

7. At the right of 'Your Membership', tap the Active button to open the Apple Music Membership screen

8. In the Renewal Options section, select the required subscription plan and then tap the Subscribe button

Having signed up for the free trial or one of the subscription plans, you will see the 'Tell us what you like' screen shown below:

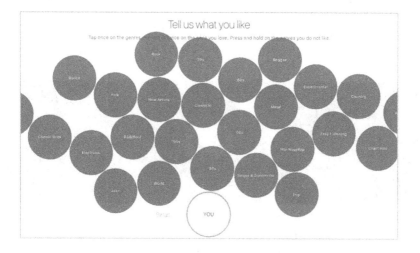

1. Select the periods, genre, singers, etc and then tap Next at the top-right

2. In the next screen select your favorites and then tap Done at the top-right

3. After a short period, you will be presented with a range of music based on your selections in Steps 1 and 2

4. To play a song just tap on it to reveal the mini-player at the bottom – it will now be streamed to your iPad

5. If you would prefer to download the song to your iPad for offline listening, tap the More ⋯ button at the far-right of the song and then tap Make Available Offline. A pop-up window will open stating that you need to enable iCloud Music Library in the Settings app. To do so, tap Settings. In the Library section, toggle the iCloud Music Library switch to On

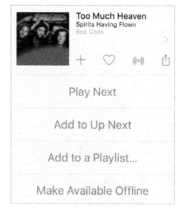

6. If you already have music on the iPad, you will then be offered options to either merge it with the music being downloaded or replace it

7. In either case, it will now be downloaded to your My Music library. To access it, tap My Music on the toolbar at the bottom of the screen

Apple Radio

Formerly iTunes Radio, Apple Music Radio provides two categories of station: pre-created stations created by Apple, and custom stations based on artists or songs that you create yourself. To access them, open the Music app and then tap Radio on the bottom toolbar. Right at the top is Beats 1, which broadcasts 24/7 to more than 100 countries. Tap the Listen Now button to start it up.

Scroll down and, below the Featured Stations section, you will see the pre-created stations. These cover a range of genres as we see below:

As mentioned above, you also have the option of creating your own customized radio stations. To do this:

1. Open the Music app

2. Find the song or artist you want to base the station on

3. Tap the More ⋯ button at the far-right of the song

4. On the menu that opens, select 'Start Station'

5. A new station based on the song or artist will be created

CHAPTER 10

Reading

E-books have arrived and are here to stay. While they will never completely replace physical books, they do offer certain advantages and features that make them an interesting alternative.

For example, bookmarks mean you will never lose your page; people with poor eyesight can increase text size; you can make notes as you go along; you will never be short of something to read as long as you have a network connection, plus many more.

To find your reading material, you need to access the iBooks Store. We show you how to do this, plus how to review and download books.

Keep up With the News

Your iPad is portable and comes equipped with a high-resolution Retina screen – these two features make it an ideal device on which to read the written word. Yes, you can buy a dedicated Kindle but there is really no need – the iPad is just as good for reading, if not actually better. To this end, it comes with two reading apps – News and iBooks. We'll look at the former first.

News is a new app and replaces the Newsstand app. It is designed for use with news channels such as newspapers, magazines and websites Not only does the app enable you to read them, it also helps you to manage them so you can quickly see what you have available to read at any time.

1. Tap the News app to open it

2. After the Welcome screen and privacy disclaimer, you'll see a Get Started button

3. You will now be asked to select at least one news channel; we recommend you select a few more than that in order to get a variety of articles. However, you can add more channels, at any time. Everything you select will be added to your Favorites

4. When you've made your selections, the app generates what is in effect a customized magazine that pulls its content from all the sources you have specified. This can be accessed at any time by tapping the For You button on the Options bar at the bottom-left of the screen

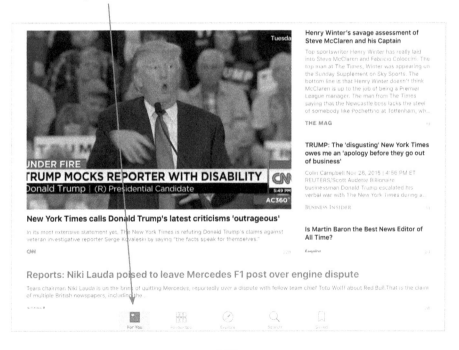

cont'd

To read an article, just tap on it. When you have article open, you'll see a heart shaped icon at the top-right. Tap it and the News app will endeavour to find and present similar articles in future.

The Options bar has four other buttons: Favorites, Explore, Search, and Saved. Tap Favorites to see a list of all the channels you selected when setting up the app. To add more, use the Search app to locate them. Having found one, tap the outlet to open it and then tap the + button at the top-right.

You can remove channels from your Favorites by tapping Edit at the top-right – this places an X on all the channels. To remove one, tap the X. Tapping the Explore button opens a list of suggested channels and topics for your consideration – these cover a wide range of topics including News, Sport, Business, Politics, Travel, Technology, Science, Entertainment and Food.

Finally, the Save button shows all the articles you have saved for later perusal. Articles can be placed here as follows:

1. Using For You, Explore, or Search, find an article you want to save

2. Tap and hold on the article until you see the pop-up menu shown below:

3. Tap the Save button

Other options on the menu include Share Story, which lets you share it via email, social media, etc; and Mute Channel, which stops further articles from the channel appearing.

The iBooks App

When it comes to reading books on your iPad, the iBooks app is where you need to go. This app enables you to download and store literally hundreds of books across all genres on your iPad. They can then be read whether you're at home, on a plane or on a ship – it acts as your own personal, portable, library.

Get started by:

1. Open the iBooks app

2. The app opens in the All Books view. If you haven't bought any books yet, the view is empty. When you have, they are displayed as shown below:

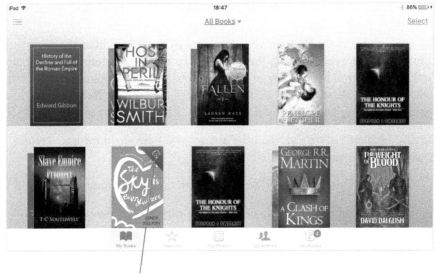

3. If you see a book with a cloud icon at the top-right corner, it means the book hasn't yet been downloaded to the iPad. To do so, just tap once on the book. Any books without the cloud icon are already on the iPad

4. A blue New banner at the top-right corner of a book indicates that it hasn't been opened yet

At the top and bottom of the screen are a number of icons and links. Working clockwise from top-left, these are:

*   ☰ – this lets you view your library in a number of ways. These include Most Recent, Titles, Authors, and Categories, and can be selected from the menu bar at the top of the screen

*   **All Books** – this opens a menu that lets you view your books in categories or collections. Default collections are All (everything in the library), Books (just the books), Audiobooks, and PDFs

- **Select** – tap Select to open the Select Items page. This lets you select books individually, or collectively by tapping Select All.

Having done so, you then have two choices: You can tap Move to open the Collections list and select a different collection in which to move the book.

Or you can tap Delete to delete the book. Note only books that are actually on the iPad can be deleted. If you select a book that is in the Cloud, the Delete option will not be available

Also, deleting a book will not remove it from the collection – it will still be there but will now have the cloud icon at the top-right corner indicating it is now in the Cloud.

If you don't want to see the book in the collection at all, tap the 'Hide iCloud Books' switch at the bottom of the Collections menu to On

Also on the Collections menu is a '+ New Collection' option. This lets you organize your book library by creating your own collections and naming them appropriately. Having done so, you can then move existing books to these collections as described above

At the bottom of the iBooks screen is a toolbar. This offers the following options:

- **Purchased** – located at the far-right of the toolbar, this shows you two views of your library: the first is All, and the second is 'Not on This iPad', i.e. books that are on the Cloud

- **Top Authors** – this opens an alphabetical list of authors, both paid and free. Tap on an author's name to see which of their books are available for download

- **Top Charts** – see what books are currently in the best-seller charts. You can peruse a separate list for both paid and free books, plus audiobooks

- **Featured** – a list of selected titles that may appeal to you

- **My Books** – this takes you to your book shelf where your books are listed

Finding Books

To find books to download to your iPad, your first port of call is the iBooks Store. To access the Store, open the iBooks app and select either 'Top Authors', 'Top Charts', or 'Featured' from the toolbar at the bottom.

All three options show a different view of the store. Below, we see the Featured view:

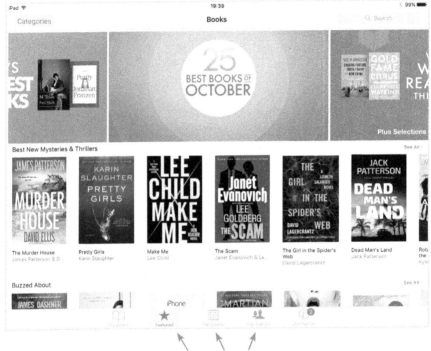

Use these buttons on the toolbar to search for books

If you are looking for something specific, it will probably be quicker to use the search box at the top-right of the screen.

Note that you are not restricted to the iBooks Store for your reading material. The iBooks app supports the EPUB format, which is used by many online book stores. For example, go to www.epubbooks.com and you will find an excellent selection of books that are in the public domain, i.e. are free.

You can also read Kindle books on your iPad. However, this cannot be done with the iBooks app – you will have to download and install the Kindle app. Once done though, your entire Kindle library will be available on it.

The same applies to books purchased from the Barnes & Noble bookstore. Just install the Barnes & Noble app to read them on your iPad.

Previewing & Downloading Books

Having found a book that might be of interest, you now need to look a bit closer before opening your wallet:

1. Tap on the book to open its Details page

2. Tap Reviews to see what other readers think of the book

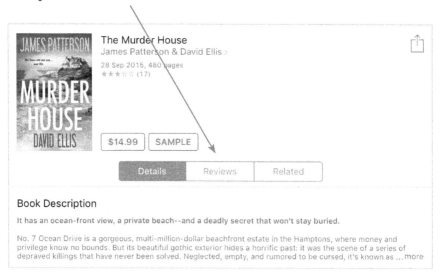

3. If you want to read an excerpt of the book before committing yourself, tap the SAMPLE button – a short sample will be downloaded to the iPad and can be accessed in the iBooks app

4. When you are sure you want the book, tap the price button and then the Buy Book button. Enter your password in the iTunes Store login screen and then tap OK

5. The purchase is charged to the credit card registered to your Apple account and the book is then downloaded to your iPad

6. Tap My Books at the bottom-left of the screen and you will see the newly downloaded book at the top-left of your book shelf

Reading Books

Unlike a physical book where what you see is what you get, with e-books there are a number of options that let you control the book, and also tailor the display for a better reading experience. Open the iBooks app and then select the book you want to read from your library. Then use the following options to read and control the book:

- **View a single page** – hold the iPad in Portrait mode

- **View two pages** – hold the iPad in Landscape mode

- **Turn to the next page** – either tap the right-hand side of the screen or flick to the left of the page with your finger

- **Turn to the previous page** – either tap the left-hand side of the screen or flick to the right of the page with your finger

- **Revealing the controls** – tap anywhere on the screen to reveal the controls – tap on the screen again to conceal them

- **Scroll up and down through the pages** – reveal the controls and tap the Fonts ᴀA button at the top-right. Then tap Scrolling View

- **Bookmarks** – to bookmark a page, reveal the controls and tap the Bookmarks ⌑ button at the top-right

- **Accessing the library** – reveal the controls and tap Library at the top

- **Open the Table of Contents** – tap on the screen to reveal the controls and then tap the Contents ☰ button

- **Move about in the book** – tap on the screen to reveal the controls and then, at the bottom of the screen, drag the dot on the slider left or right

- **Search the book for a specific word or page number** – tap on the screen to reveal the controls and then tap the Search ⌕ button at the top right of the screen

E-Books and Text

The iBooks app provides you with a number of ways to view, alter and search the text in any book. You can also look up dictionary definitions and make notes as you go along. Lets take a look at the available options:

Formatting Text

Text in all books uses a specific font – a set of printable or displayable characters in a specific style and size. With a physical book, the font cannot be changed but in an e-book, it can.

One of the most useful changes that can be made is the size of the font. For example, people with poor eyesight can increase it to a level that makes it much easier for them to read. To do this, and more:

1. Open the book and tap on the screen to reveal the controls

2. Tap on the Fonts ᴀA button

3. Tap the small A to reduce the size of the font, and the large A to increase it

4. To change the font itself, tap on the Fonts line. This opens a pop-up giving you eight fonts from which to choose

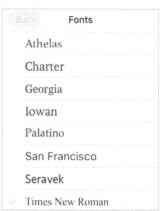

5. The Fonts menu offers some other options as well. Right at the top is a control that lets you alter the brightness of the screen

6. Further down is a screen color control that lets you change the screen color to White, Sepia, Gray or Black. White is the default color but we recommend using Sepia instead as it is easier on the eye

7. Finally, there is a Auto-Night Theme option. This is designed to reduce excessive glare that can be the cause of eye strain. It uses your location and time to detect when daylight is over and automatically switch to the Night theme – a black background with light grey text

cont'd

When reading an e-book, tapping and holding on a word opens a toolbar that offers a number of options as we see below:

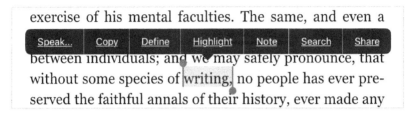

These include speaking the word, defining it, highlighting it, searching for other instances, and making notes related to the word. Lets see how these work:

- **Speak...** – if you're not sure how the word is pronounced, tap 'Speak...' (if you don't see it on the toolbar, enable the option as we explain on the next page). The iPad will now speak the word to you

- **Define** – if you aren't sure of the meaning of the word, tap Define. This opens a dictionary definition of the word – you will also see an option for searching the Web.

  If you don't get a definition, it is because there is no dictionary on the iPad. Tap Manage to access a list of dictionaries and tap the one you want – it will now be downloaded to your iPad

- **Highlight** – this offers a number of options such as color and underline with which you can highlight the word

- **Note** – this option lets you make a note at the selected point in the book for later reference. A blank note will appear and the keyboard will open at the bottom – type your note. The word will then be highlighted and a yellow square placed in the margin alongside the line in which the word is located. To read the note, just tap on the square

  You can review all your notes and bookmarks by opening the Table of Contents page as described on page 172. On the toolbar at the top, you"ll see the Notes and Bookmarks buttons

Let the iPad Read to You

We saw on the previous page how you can get your iPad to speak words to you. Well, it can actually do a lot more than this – it can read an entire book. The feature that enables this is an accessibility feature called Speech, which we took a brief look at on page 63.

To set this up:

1. Tap the Settings app

2. Go to General > Accessibility > Speech

3. Tap the Speak Screen switch to the On position

4. Open the book at the page you want to start reading from and drag downwards from the top of the screen with two fingers

5. The iPad now starts reading the book aloud. At the same time, an iBooks toolbar appears on the screen as shown below:

Options on the toolbar include Minimize, Speak Slower, Go back a Page, Pause/Play, Go Forward a Page, Speak Faster, and Close.

While you have the Speech settings screen open, you can set the iPad to speak with a foreign accent by selecting a language – tap Voices to set this. You can also adjust the speed at which it reads by adjusting the Speaking Rate slider.

Use Your iPad as a Kindle

One of the biggest gripes from Kindle users is that the devices do not provide a color screen. They are also a touch on the small side. However, both of these issues can be resolved by using your iPad as a Kindle.

How? – all you have to do is install the Kindle app, which is available as a free download from the App Store. Furthermore, if you already have a Kindle account, you can import your existing Kindle books to your iPad.

To do it:

1. Open the App Store and enter 'kindle for ipad' in the search box at the top-right of the screen

2. In the search results, tap on the Kindle icon to download and install it on your iPad

3. Go to the end of your Home screen and tap the Kindle app to open it

4. In the 'Register this Kindle' screen, enter your email address and password

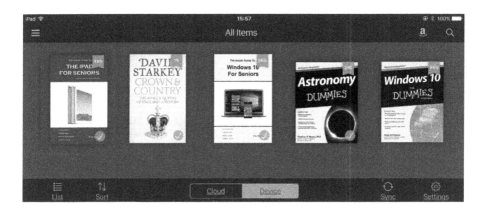

When the main screen opens, you'll see a tab bar at the bottom. Tapping the Cloud tab will show all your Kindle books (if any). Just tap on one to download it to the iPad. When the download is complete, tap it again to open the book. If you tap the Device tab, you'll see all the books that are actually on the iPad.

At the top-left of the screen, tap the ▤ button. This opens a menu that provides a number of options. Tap the ⓐ button at the top-right right to open the Kindle book store from where you can buy books, periodicals and magazines and download them to your iPad.

CHAPTER 11

Security

If you are like most other users, it won't be long before your iPad is jam-packed with information and data that is either highly personal and thus confidential, or simply too important to lose – indeed, maybe both.

To protect your data, the device provides a number of security features. These include password protection, backing up, and protection controls. In this chapter, we explain how to configure and use these features in order to keep your data safe and secure.

Locking Your iPad

If you need to restrict access to your iPad for whatever reason, you have two options:

Touch ID

Introduced with the iPad Air 2, Touch ID employs a biometric fingerprint scanner that is built-in to the Home button. This takes a picture of your fingerprint when you touch the button, which is then analyzed. If it matches the fingerprint taken when Touch ID was set up, the iPad is unlocked.

The feature also requires a four- or six-digit passcode to be specified during the setup procedure. This is used for backup purposes should Touch ID fail to open the iPad or need to be reconfigured.

The Touch ID setup procedure is part of the initial iPad setup wizard as we mentioned on pages 52-53. However, you can set it up at any time by following the instructions on the next two pages.

Passcode

If you don't want to use Touch ID, you can instead just use a passcode to secure your iPad. You will need to enter it when:

- Switching on, or restarting, the iPad

- Sliding to unlock the screen

- Updating your iPad's software

- Erasing the iPad's content

Note: if you enter the wrong passcode six times in a row, you'll be locked out and a message will say that your iPad is disabled. You'll then have to erase the iPad completely and set it up again from scratch. This will, of course, delete all your third-party apps, data and settings.

Touch ID

Pro, Air 2, and Mini 4 iPads all come with fingerprint recognition technology built-in to the Home button. Just touch the button with a finger and your device will be unlocked automatically. You can also use the feature for making purchases in the App Store, the iTunes Store and the iBooks Store.

Note, however, that a passcode is still required. While Touch ID is designed to minimize the need to use the passcode, it will be required for additional security validation, such as enrolling new fingerprints or making changes in the feature's settings.

Set Up Touch ID
Setting up Touch ID fingerprint recognition is quite a protracted procedure, particularly if you set up more than one finger. To do it:

1. Open the Settings app

2. On the left-hand side of the screen, tap 'Touch ID & Passcode'

3. On the Enter Passcode screen, specify a passcode. Confirm it on the next screen

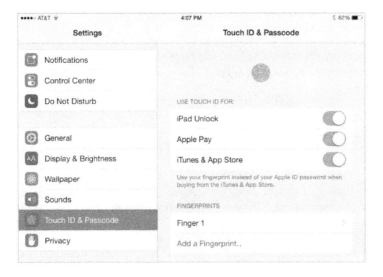

4. Tap 'Add a Fingerprint'

5. Touch the finger you want to use to the Home button and then follow the prompts to scan in your fingerprint

    Repeat this procedure for all the fingers you want to use with Touch ID. If other people will be using the feature as well but aren't currently available, they can always add their fingerprint later on

Using Touch ID to Unlock the iPad

The beauty of Touch ID is that you can unlock your iPad without having to enter a passcode every time. This can be done in two ways:

● Press the Home button to wake your iPad and keep your finger on it

● Press the Sleep/Wake button to wake your iPad, and then touch the Home button

If Touch ID doesn't recognize your finger, you'll be asked to try again. After five unsuccessful attempts, you'll be asked to enter your passcode. You'll also need to enter your passcode to unlock the iPad in the following situations:

● After restarting the iPad

● When more than 48 hours have elapsed since the last time you unlocked the iPad

● To enter the Touch ID & Passcode settings screen

Using Touch ID for the iTunes, App and iBooks Stores

You can use Touch ID instead of entering your Apple ID password to buy content from the above-mentioned stores.

First though, make sure that iTunes & App Store is turned on in Settings > Touch ID & Passcode.

When done, make purchases with Touch ID by following these steps:

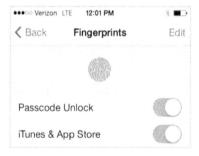

1. Browse to the required item in the chosen Store

2. Tap the item you wish to purchase – instead of the Apple ID password prompt, you'll see a Touch ID prompt

3. Touch the Home button with a scanned finger. You'll need to do this for each purchase

4. If the fingerprint checks out, the purchase is completed without further ado

If Touch ID doesn't recognize your finger, you'll be asked to try again. After five failed attempts, you'll be given the option to enter your Apple ID password (not the Touch ID passcode, note).

Passcode

iOS 8 required a four-digit passcode. iOS 9 lets you increase the security level of your iPad by offering the option to set a six-digit passcode. To set this up:

1. Open the Settings app

2. On the right-hand side, tap Touch ID & Passcode (on iPad's without Touch ID, tap Passcode)

3. Tap 'Turn Passcode On'

4. Enter a four-digit passcode. Alternatively, tap Passcode Options to switch to set a six-digit passcode

5. Re-enter the passcode to confirm it and then tap Done

From now on, the 'Slide to unlock' button at the bottom of the Lock screen will open a keypad – tap in the passcode and your iPad will be unlocked. If you already have a four-digit passcode set and want to change it to a six-digit one, do the following:

1. Acess the passcode setting screen as explained above

2. Tap Change Passcode

3. Enter the existing passcode when prompted

4. Tap Passcode Options

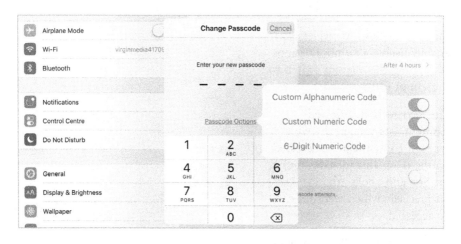

5. Tap the 6-digit Numeric Code option and then enter your six numbers.

Note that you also have options to set a custom numeric code, or a custom alphanumeric code.

Content Restriction

For many users, it won't really be necessary to lock other people out of their iPad, and so have to go to the bother of setting up Touch ID or using a passcode.

If all you want to do is restrict certain actions and/or access to certain types of data, there is an iPad setting called Restrictions (also known as Parental Controls) that allows you to specify precisely what content can and can't be accessed on your iPad.

It enables you to block apps such as Safari, Camera, and FaceTime, functions such as Siri and AirDrop, and access to the iTunes, iBooks, and App Stores. Content can be blocked by age and rating, as can the ability to make changes to accounts and app settings.

With regard to children, Restrictions provides a way to block access to anything and everything you deem inappropriate for them.

To set up Restrictions:

1. Open the Settings app and then tap General

2. Scroll down to and tap Restrictions

3. You will notice that the restrictions are grayed-out so they cannot be selected. To make them selectable, tap Enable Restrictions

4. When prompted, enter your passcode and confirm it in the next screen. The restrictions will now be available for selection

The first section, Allow, lets you enable/disable a number of apps by tapping the relevant switch to the On or Off position.

The next section, Allowed Content, lets you specify what types of content can be accessed on the iPad. This includes music, movies, and books. You can also set precisely which websites can be accessed.

The Privacy and Allow Changes sections let you prevent unauthorized changes to certain apps and functions.

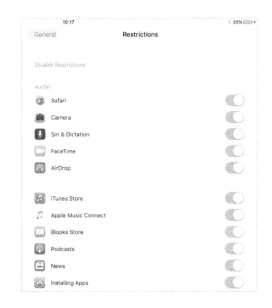

Backing Up Your iPad

Having configured your iPad to prevent or restrict unauthorized access, you now need to consider the security of your data. This can be compromised in a number of ways – loss of the iPad, accidental deletion, and viruses being typical examples.

The best way of protecting against these scenarios is to make a complete backup of everything on the device. There are two ways to do this: backup to the Cloud, i.e. your iCloud account, or to a computer. Our recommendation is that you go with the former option as this means you can also restore the backup from the Cloud – a connection to a computer is not needed at all.

Backup to the Cloud
This requires you to have an iCloud account. If you don't, set one up as previously described. Then:

1. Open the Settings app and then tap iCloud on the left of the screen

2. Scroll down to and tap Backup

3. Tap the iCloud Backup switch to the On position

4. Enter your enter your Apple password when prompted

5. Tap 'Back Up Now'

Backup to a Computer
This method requires the use of iTunes which, of course, means you have to connect the iPad to the computer. When you have:

1. Start iTunes

2. At the top-left under the menu bar, click the iPad button

3. On the right, you'll see a Backups section. Here, you'll see options for automatically backing up to iCloud and to This computer

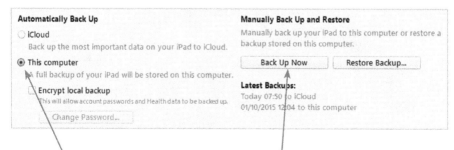

4. Select the This Computer option and then click 'Back Up Now'

Restoring Your iPad

How you go about restoring your iPad from a backup depends on where the backup is located.

Restore From the Cloud

If your backup was done directly from the iPad and saved in the Cloud, the restoration procedure is:

1. Open the Settings app and then go to General. On the right, scroll down to, and tap, Reset

2. Tap 'Erase All Content And Settings' and then enter your passcode

3. Tap Erase in the pop-up window

4. When the existing data has been deleted, you'll be taken to the setup assistant you saw when first setting up the iPad – tap 'Setup Your Device'

5. Tap 'Restore From a backup'

6. Sign in to iCloud

7. Select the backup you want to use for the restore procedure

Restore From a Computer

First, connect the iPad to the computer on which the backup is stored. Having done so, follow the steps below:

1. Open iTunes and, at the top-left under the menu bar, click the iPad button

2. On the right, you'll see a Backups section. Under 'Manually Backup and Restore', click 'Restore Backup...'

3. In the new window, select a backup to restore from

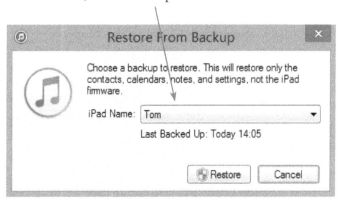

4. Click the Restore button

Locating & Protecting a Lost iPad

The iPad is a relatively small device and, like all small devices, is easily lost or stolen. As it is quite likely to contain a lot of stuff you'd rather other people didn't see, losing the device can be a bit of a mini crisis.

You may be reassured to know therefore, that should this happen to you there are steps you can take to not only locate the iPad but also to remotely disable it, or even delete everything on it.

The Find My iPhone App

To discover where a missing iPad is located, you need to use an app called Find My iPhone. You will also need the use of an iPhone, a different iPad, or an iPod Touch that has the Find My iPhone app installed on it. If a suitable device isn't available, you can always access the Find My iPhone app via your online iCloud account.

The app works by looking for a signal that the iPad beams out. However, you should be aware that, by default, this signal is turned off. So if you envisage ever having to use Find My iPhone, you must activate the signal on your iPad beforehand:

1. Open the Settings app

2. On the left of the screen, tap iCloud

3. Tap the 'Find My iPad' switch to the On position

Using the Find My iPhone App to Find a Lost iPad

The steps outlined below will enable you to pinpoint the location of a missing iPad on a map:

1. On another device containing the Find My iPhone app, launch the app – you will be prompted to enter your Apple ID and password

2. The app signs in to your Apple account

3. You'll now see a list of devices the app has found – tap on your missing iPad

4. The app displays the location of your iPad on a map. You can zoom in for a closer look

5. At the bottom of the screen tap Actions to reveal three options: Play Sound, Lost Mode and Erase iPad

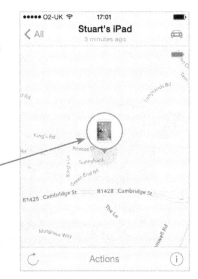

- **Play Sound** – if you tap Play Sound, the iPad will play a sound for two minutes, assuming it is switched on and connected to a network. Typically, you'll use this option if you know the device has simply been misplaced

- **Lost Mode** – tap Lost Mode if you want to lock your iPad to prevent unauthorized access. This option also lets you send a phone number where you can be reached to the iPad, plus place a message on it

- **Erase iPad** – the nuclear option to be used when all else has failed. This will remove all data from the iPad

Using the Find My iPhone App on Your iCloud Account
If you don't have another Apple device, you won't be able to use the method outlined above to track and disable your iPad. In this case, you need to go online:

1. Login to your iCloud account at www.icloud.com

2. Sign-in with your Apple password

3. Click Find iPhone

4. A map will open showing the location of your various Apple devices (assuming you have more than one). To see the location of a specific device, select it from the All Devices menu at the top of the screen. At the bottom of the screen, you will see the Play Sound, Lost Mode and Erase iPad options

CHAPTER 12
iCloud & Related Services

So far, we have taken an in-depth look at the main applications provided by the iPad and associated apps – email (Mail app), the Internet (Safari), pictures (Photos app), video (Videos app), music (Music app) and reading (iBooks app).

In this chapter, we will take a look at Apple's iCloud feature that allows users to store, share, and access their data in the cloud, i.e. on an Apple server.

We'll also look at various related services offered by Apple that rely on the use of iCloud.

What is Cloud Computing?

We mention the Cloud and, more specifically, iCloud, quite a few times in this book. What do these two terms mean though?

The Cloud

The Cloud or, to give it its full title, Cloud Computing, is a term that describes the storing and access of data on the Internet rather than on a computer's hard drive – the term 'Cloud' is simply a metaphor for the Internet. It originates from the days when, in flowcharts and presentations, the Internet was represented as a fluffy white cumulus cloud.

Cloud computing does not involve the hard drive on your computer at all. Also, it has nothing to do with having your own dedicated hardware server; storing and accessing data on a home or office network is not classed as using the Cloud. To be classified as cloud computing, data and programs *must* be stored and accessed on the Internet. More specifically, for the Internet read server farm – these consist of hundreds of computers and store huge amounts of data.

Two well known examples of cloud computing include:

- **Google Drive** – provided by Google, this is a service that lets you do your computing almost entirely on the Internet. The programs, or apps, and the data storage are all online – the only thing you need provide is a means of accessing the service. This can be a computer, tablet or smartphone

- **Amazon Cloud Drive** – very similar to Google Drive, Amazon Cloud Drive provides free online storage up to a limit of 5 GB – any more than that and you have to start paying. You also get free apps that allow you to access your data from any device, anywhere

iCloud

A third example of cloud computing, and one of the best known, is Apple's iCloud service. This started out as a simple online storage and data synchronization service but has rapidly expanded to provide a host of other related services. These include:

- iCloud Automatic Data Synchronization
- iCloud Drive
- Family Sharing
- iTunes Match
- iCloud Keychain
- iCloud Photo Sharing
- iCloud Photo Library

We'll now take a closer look at these iCloud services and see what they have to offer to iPad users.

iCloud Automatic Data Synchronization

We've seen several examples of how you can synchronize various types of data, such as your contacts list, between your computer and the iPad. This is done with the iTunes program on the computer and saves you having to laboriously enter the data manually on to the iPad. Thankfully, once you've got your data on the device, keeping it updated is just as easy – this is courtesy of iCloud and is known as automatic data synchronization.

Once you've set up iCloud on your iPad, auto-synchronization kicks in immediately. It sends your email, along with your contacts, calendars, reminders, notes, and Safari bookmarks, to its central online server. Photo Stream, too, starts automatically uploading any photos you have taken.

From the server, it is then sent to all your other iOS devices. So if you also have an iPhone, all the data on the iPad will be accessible on the iPhone. The same applies to data created on the iPhone – it is sent to the central server and from there is sent to your iPad and other devices. For example, if you make a note with the Note app on your iPad, you can read, edit or delete it with the Note app on your iPhone.

Before you can use iCloud, it must be set up:

1. Open the Settings app and, on the left-hand side, tap iCloud

2. If you already have an Apple ID, enter the details and tap Sign In

3. If you don't, tap 'Create a New Apple ID' and follow the prompts

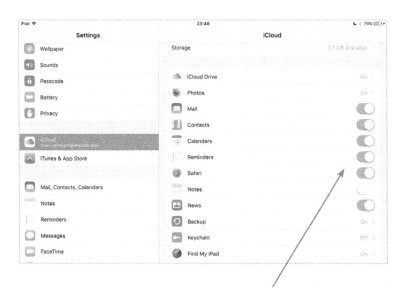

4. Once iCloud is set up, you can specify the types of data you want to sync by tapping the relevant switches to On or Off

iCloud Drive

iCloud Drive is Apple's version of Dropbox. It's basically a document-oriented file storage service that keeps your data in sync between your various devices. It is very similar to iCloud but lets you store and synchronize all types of data and documents whereas iCloud limits you to certain types of data as we explained on the previous page.

With iCloud Drive, you get up to 5 GB of sttorage space for free. If you need more than this, paid storage plans are available ranging from 20 GB to 1 TB.

With your iCloud Drive, you can:

● Store and access all types of document in one central location

● Keep files and folders up-to-date across all your devices

● Create new files and folders from iCloud-enabled apps

● Work on the same file across multiple apps. Any changes made to a document on one device automatically appear on all your other devices

● Access your files on the go from the iCloud Drive app

If you want to use iCloud Drive with your iPad, you need to switch it on. To do this:

1. Open the Settings app

2. Tap iCloud on the left-hand side

3. Tap iCloud Drive and then tap the iCloud Drive switch to On

Note that any compatible documents you've already stored in iCloud will now be moved automatically to iCloud Drive. Also, remember to set up iCloud Drive on any other devices you intend to use with it.

To access documents on your iCloud Drive:

1. Using any web browser, go to www.icloud.com and sign in with your Apple ID and password

2. On a Mac running OS X Yosemite, go to iCloud Drive in Finder

3. On a Windows computer running Windows 7 or later, go to File Explorer > iCloud Drive

4. On your iPad, iPhone, or iPod Touch, your documents can be accessed from Apple apps such as Pages, Numbers and Keynote, and any non-Apple apps that support iCloud Drive

Family Sharing

Family Sharing is a feature that makes it possible to share your data with other people. Data that can be shared includes:

- Apps, photos, movies, home videos, music, and e-books

- Your location

- Scheduled events on a family calendar

Setting Up Family Sharing

Before you can use Family Sharing, the feature must be set up and people invited to participate. Do it as described in the following steps:

1. On the Home screen, tap the Settings app

2. Tap iCloud

3. Tap 'Set Up Family Sharing...'

4. Tap Get Started

5. Tap Continue. Note that one person must be in charge of Family Sharing, i.e. organize it, and this will be the person who sets it up. The Family Sharing account will be linked to that persons Apple ID

6. In the next screen, you agree that family members will be able to share iTunes, iBooks and App Store purchases made using your account. If you are happy with this, tap Continue

   If you are not, at the bottom of the screen, you will see an option that allows you to specify a different account from which to share purchases

7. You will now see a notice stating that you agree to pay for all purchases initiated by family members with the credit card registered to the specified account. Tap Continue

8. You will be asked if you want to share your location with your family. Tap either Share Location or Not Now

9. Family Sharing is now created and you are taken to the Family Members screen in the iCloud section of the Settings App

10. Tap 'Add Family Member...'. An email window will open – enter the email address of the person you want to invite and then tap Next to send the invitation. You can invite any number of people in this way

11. You will now see the person you have just invited listed under Family Members. However, he or she will have to accept the invitation before they can take part in Family Sharing

12. Should you ever wish to stop a particular person from participating in Family Sharing, tap their name under Family Members and then tap Remove

Note: to be able to use Family Sharing, invited family members must have an iPad, iPhone or iPod Touch running iOS 8 or iOS 9, or a Mac computer running OS X Yosemite.

Sharing Content

With Family Sharing set up, you can now start sharing various types of data. For example, open the Calendar app and then tap Calendars at the bottom of the screen – you will now see a Family calendar. Select it and then enter an event you want to share. The event will be added to the Family calendar and other members of the Family Sharing group will be sent a notification advising a new event has been posted. It will be visible on the Family calendar on their devices.

In the Photos app, tap the Shared button at the bottom. You will now see a Family photo album. Open the album, tap the + button at the top-left and the choose the pictures to add to the album. Then tap Done. Make sure the Family album is selected as the Shared Album and then tap Post. The selected pictures will now be available for viewing by all members of the Family Sharing group.

Note: to be able to share photos with Family Sharing, you must enable iCloud Photo Sharing as described on page 152.

Members of a Family Sharing group can also share purchases from the iTunes Store, the App Store and the iBooks Store. Open the required store and tap the Purchased button at the bottom of the screen. Then tap My Purchases at the top-left of the screen

Tap on a member to open a list of the purchases they have made. If you want to download an item to your iPad, just tap the cloud icon to the right of it.

iTunes Match

iTunes Match is a paid subscription service offered by Apple. The basic premise is that it lets you store your entire music collection in the Cloud. This includes music you have uploaded to your iPad from your computer and music you have bought from the iTunes Store. As it is located in the Cloud, the music can be accessed on all your devices.

How it Works

During the setup procedure, iTunes scans the music on your iPad to see if any of it is available in the iTunes Store. Any songs that are, i.e. 'match' are automatically uploaded from the Store to the Cloud. Songs that aren't in the Store are uploaded from the iPad itself. Because the vast majority of your music will be in the Store (it contains some 43 million songs), the upload procedure is thus much faster than uploading all the songs from your iPad.

Once uploaded to the Cloud, you can listen to your music on an iPhone, iPad, iPod Touch, Mac, computer and Apple TV. There are provisos though:

- iTunes Match is limited to 25,000 songs

- Songs larger than 200 MB will not be uploaded

- Songs longer than two hours will not be uploaded

- Songs encrypted with Digital Rights Management (DRM) will not be matched or uploaded unless your device is authorized for playback of that content

A cool feature of iTunes Match is that the service will automatically upgrade any low-quality music files you have uploaded to a much higher quality level. If you decide to download these high-quality files to your device, they are yours to keep even if you subsequently let your iTunes Match subscription expire.

Setting Up iTunes Match

If you are interested in giving iTunes Match a go on your iPad, you can set it up as detailed below:

1. Open the Settings app

2. Scroll down to and tap Music on the left-hand side of the screen

3. Tap 'Subscribe to iTunes Match' on the right

4. You might be asked to validate your billing information. After you've added a valid payment method, tap Subscribe

5. Payment will be taken after which you are ready to go

iCloud Keychain

iCloud Keychain is an Apple password management system. With it, your account names, passwords, and credit card numbers can be safely stored and synced across all your devices. In conjunction with Safari, they can be used to autofill login and credit card number fields.

Setting Up iCloud Keychain

To get started with iCloud Keychain:

1. Open the Settings app

2. Tap iCloud on the left of the screen

3. Tap Keychain on the right and then tap the switch to On

4. You are presented with two options: 'Use 'iCloud Security Code' and 'Create Different Code'. If you select the former, you will be asked to enter the passcode you use to unlock your iPad.

   If you select the latter, you will be asked to create a different passcode. In both cases, you will then be asked to specify a phone number that is capable of receiving text messages. Then tap Next – job done

Saving Passwords and Credit Cards

Although it is now activated, you can't use your Keychain yet. You first need to turn on some settings in Safari:

1. Open the Settings app

2. Scroll down to and tap Safari on the left-hand side of the screen

3. In the General section on the right, tap AutoFill

4. Tap both 'Names and Passwords' and 'Credit Cards' to On

5. Tap 'Saved Credit Cards' and then enter your iPad passcode when prompted

6. Tap 'Add Credit Card' and then enter the card's details in the next screen

The next time you go to a password-protected site in Safari and enter the password, you will be offered the option of saving the password so that the next time you visit the site, the password field will be filled in automatically.

The same applies to your credit card – from now on, you will never have to enter the number manually.

iCloud Photo Sharing

Your iPad's iCloud Photo Sharing feature is designed to not only let you share a designated photo album with your friends, but to also let them add their own pictures to the album.

To set up iCloud Photo Sharing:

1. Open the Settings app and tap iCloud at the left of the screen

2. Tap Photos on the right and then tap 'iCloud Photo Sharing' to On

3. Close the Settings app and now open the Photos app

4. Tap Shared at the bottom and then tap 'New Shared Album...'

5. Type a name for your shared album and tap Next

6. Enter the email addresses of all the people you want to share the album with. If you tap the + button at the right, you can select them from your contacts list

7. Tap Create

8. In the Photos app, open the newly created album and then tap the gray square to open the Moments group

9. Select the pictures and videos you want to share and then tap Done

10. In the pop-up window, type an accompanying note if you want to and then tap Post at the top-right

In the meantime, your invited friends will have received an email containing a 'Subscribe' link. If they click the link, they will be able to view the shared album on their device and add pictures to it themselves. However, if you'd rather that your friends didn't add their own pictures, you can prevent them from doing so by opening the shared album on your iPad and tapping People at the top-right. This opens an editing screen offering several options.

One of them is 'Subscribers Can Post'. Tap this to Off. Other options let you invite more people to share the album, plus a public website option that lets absolutely anyone view the album.

Pictures and videos stored in Photo Sharing albums do not count with regard to your free 5 GB iCloud data allowance. However, a shared album can hold a maximum of 5000 pictures and videos combined.

iCloud Photo Library

iCloud Photo Library is Apple's latest cloud-based service. Its purpose is to enable users to move their entire photo and video libraries into the Cloud, thus saving space on their iPad and, at the same time, enabling them to seamlessly sync their pictures and videos across all their iOS devices.

When enabled, iCloud Photo Library replaces the Camera Roll and the My Photo Stream album with an All Photos album in the Photos app. It also removes the 30 day restriction on pictures stored in My Photo Stream.

The service uses your free 5 GB iCloud storage space to store the pictures. If your photo collection requires more space than this, you will have to take out a subscription plan.

With this in mind, the iCloud Photo Library service offers a nice feature called 'Optimize iPad Storage'. This helps you make the most of the storage space on your iPad (or other iOS device) by storing the original high-resolution pictures and videos on the Cloud, and keeping optimized low-resolution versions on your device that are also perfectly sized for it.

To turn on iCloud Photo Library:

1. Open the Settings app and tap iCloud on the left

2. Tap Photos on the right

3. Tap the iCloud Photo Library switch to On

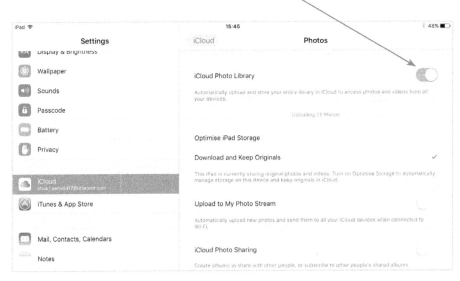

4. If you want to make use of the Optimize feature to manage your photo library, tap 'Optimize iPad Storage'

CHAPTER 13

Useful Third-Party Apps

The apps supplied with the iPad cover all the main applications that the device can be used for, e.g. email, Internet, listening to music, reading, etc. However, there are alternatives to all of them, many of which provide more, and better, features and options.

Then, of course, there are the applications that the default apps don't cover. Things like holidays, travel, property, finance and so on. In this chapter, we take a look at some third-party apps that may be useful to you.

Alternatives to Default iPad Apps

Here, we are going to look at alternatives to two of the iPad's most used default apps – the email app, Mail and the Internet app, Safari. We'll begin with Mail.

CloudMagic – with a very light and clean design, CloudMagic is a very popular email app. It offers a unified inbox that lets you see all your email from multiple accounts in one view. You can use gestures to manage your mail, and select multiple conversations to be archived or deleted.

The app supports Gmail, Microsoft Exchange, Outlook, Yahoo Mail, iCloud and IMAP accounts. It also has a passcode feature that lets you keep your email private – this is something that many users will appreciate.

Gmail – the Gmail app works in the same way as Gmail does on the Web. If you use the tabbed inbox setup, you can easily use the same setup in the app as it separates your email into Primary, Social, Promotions, Updates, and Forums. All your custom labels are available in the app as well.

You can sign into multiple Google accounts in the app and get access to your Gmail contacts to send emails. Other features include setting up a holiday responder and customizing your email signature.

Mailbox – this app aims to get emails out of your inbox as quickly as possible by placing them into categories. For each email, you're encouraged to reply if necessary, delete the message, archive it, or set it aside for later.

You can schedule messages to be returned to your inbox when you're ready to deal with them – whether it be in a few hours, days, or a specific date and time. This can be helpful for things like reservations or tickets, so you have the information you need at the appropriate time.

Boxer – if you are looking for an app that hits the middle ground between CloudMagic's power features and Mailbox's ease of use, then Boxer may just be the email app for you. It is gesture-friendly and has very handy quick-reply tools to help you clear your inbox.

Boxer lets you mark email as spam, an option not offered by other email apps. It also integrates with Evernote, Apple's Calendar app, supports Gmail labels and provides a useful to-do list.

Outlook – the official Microsoft Outlook app designed for the iPad, Outlook provides a single unified view of your email, calendar, contacts, and attachments. Swipe to quickly delete, archive, or schedule messages you want to handle later. Easily view your calendar, share available times, and schedule meetings.

Outlook works with Microsoft Exchange, Office 365, Outlook.com, iCloud, Gmail, and Yahoo Mail.

cont'd

Popular alternatives to the Safari web browsing app include:

Google Chrome – Chrome is one of the most popular alternatives for people who are linked into Google services. If you use Chrome on your Mac or PC and save bookmarks, Chrome can sync them across your devices.

You can sign in to your Google account in the app and all your settings and preferences will be available. It's also supported by many third-party apps so you can set it as the default browser.

Dolphin – if you want more of a computer browser experience on your iPad, check out Dolphin. Due to its support for gestures and the use of sidebars, the app provides a more intuitive way of browsing the web.

It offers many useful options that include a downloads manager, a choice of search engines, tab browsing and much more.

Mercury Browser Pro – Mercury Browser Pro combines the best parts of Safari and Google Chrome into one extremely powerful web browser. Features like ad blocking are built in along with passcode lock, private browsing, social network integration, and gesture support.

The app is capable of syncing bookmarks and data across all your devices with both Firefox and Chrome.

Opera Mini – Opera Mini is reckoned to be the fastest browser available. To achieve this, it crunches the size of the websites you visit by compressing images, video and text, making sites lighter and thus faster to load.

However, as a result, many of the features found in other browsers have been sacrificed. If speed is what you need though, Opera Mini is the one to go for.

Puffin – as with Opera Mini, the feature that really defines Puffin is its speed. This is achieved by compression techniques similar to those used by Opera that reduce website size.

From loading web pages to tabbing through menus, it's smooth and quick. There are also numerous add-ons to choose from, the ability to download files, and much more besides.

Atomic – Atomic is a highly flexible browser that allows the user to set up advanced privacy controls, choose from several color themes, activate an ad-blocker, customize the search engine bar, and view the source of a web page.

It also provides Facebook and Twitter integration, and features such as tabs, multi-touch gestures, passcode lock, save page, downloads and more.

Finance Apps

Finance apps include calculators, online banking, currency converters, expenditure trackers, stocks and shares monitors, and more. Some of the most popular ones include:

Debt Manager – Debt Manager helps you to organize, track, and pay off all your debts by using the Debt Snowball method, which is recognized by leading financial advisors as the most effective way to pay off multiple debts.

Loan Calculator Professional – Loan Calculator Pro is an easy-to-use financial calculator. It lets you calculate the monthly payment for different types of fixed rate loans such as home mortgage, car, and credit card.

Also, you can calculate 'what if' scenarios to determine how additional monthly and yearly payments will help you to pay off your loan earlier and save money paid in interest.

Mint – Mint is a money manager that helps you spend more sensibly and save more. Easily control all your accounts, cards and investments from one place so you can track your spending, create a budget, receive bill reminders, and get customized tips for reducing fees and saving money.

The app reviews your day-to-day spending and suggests a target so you can keep up with your lifestyle but still keep an eye how much you're spending.

HomeBudget – HomeBudget is an integrated expense tracker designed to help you track your expenses, income, bills, and account balances. It offers support for budgeting, and allows analysis of your expenses and income with charts and graphs.

Calculator for iPad Free – a very simple easy-to-use calculator that provides both normal and scientific modes. Features include a history tape that lets you save, copy and forward calculations; and a quick equation preview that displays the current equation below the result.

Stock Tracker – one of the most comprehensive stock apps, Stock Tracker brings you free streaming live quotes, pre-market/after-hour quotes, portfolio monitoring, advanced full screen charts, push notification based alerts, economic news, event/earnings calendar, market signal scans and much more.

Banking Apps – virtually all the major banks now have apps available. Many of these have implemented things like Touch ID to make them both secure and convenient. They enable you to check your balance, pay your bills, check on your mortgage, investments, credit cards, and any other financial services you may be using.

Just go to the App Store, and type your bank's name in the search box.

Property Apps

Millions of people investigate the property market from time to time. This can be to buy, rent, or just see what's available and at what price. For the iPad owner, there are a number of apps that make this easy to do right from the comfort of your favorite armchair.

Zillow – Zillow is one of the most popular property search engines in the USA. With over a million properties featured on Zillow at any one time, both for sale and to rent, you can use the Zillow app's search criteria to pinpoint the exact area you're looking to buy/rent in and specify desired features.

Just like the online site, the app lets you view floorplans, maps, local information and, of course, pictures. Any properties you save can also be synced to your laptop or computer if you so wish.

Realtor – the Realtor app lets you access and use Realtor.com, which is the official homepage of the National Association of Realtors. The site is straightforward to use and excels in providing hard facts and figures.

One of its best features is the 'Home Finance' section. Here, you can configure mortgages, home refinancing, compare fixed vs. adjustable rates, renting vs. buying, home valuation projections and more

Successful UK Property Investing – packed with loads of tips to help you with your property investing in the UK, this app helps you start your journey into the UK property market and is a useful guide when navigating your investment options.

Features include a meeting map to help you find your nearest 'pin' meeting. There is also an event calendar for property training, a forum to swap tips and lots of video advice.

Mortgage Mentor – if you're buying a house, looking to re-mortgage, or simply want to make the most of your existing mortgage, then this is the perfect app for you. It lets you try out various 'what if' scenarios and quickly see how overpayments can save you time and money.

Home Design 3D – with Home Design 3D, designing and changing your home is intuitive and quick. Whether you want to redecorate, redesign or create the home of your dreams, the app provides the means of doing so.

With literally thousands of options, including textures, shades, furniture, walls, and much much more, you can create impressive photo-realistic previews of your projects.

Travel & Holiday Apps

The iPad is the ideal device for the traveler who, depending on the destination, means of travel and reason for travel, will have need of a range of services. Apps are available for literally all these services, some of which we highlight below:

TripAdvisor – thanks to over 150 million reviews and opinions by other travelers, the TripAdvisor app makes it easy to find the lowest airfares, best hotels and restaurants, and most exciting activities, wherever you go.

App features include discovering places near your current location, getting answers to your specific travel questions in the forums plus, of course, adding your own reviews and photos. You can also download maps, reviews, and your saves for over 300 cities worldwide onto your iPad, thus avoiding the need to use expensive data roaming plans while on the move.

Skyscanner – for trips abroad, try Skyscanner. The app lets you search millions of flights from hundreds of airlines around the world – both budget and scheduled – to find the best flights at the cheapest price. When you've found your flight, it links you to the airline or travel agent so you buy directly and get the best deal – all in a few taps.

Features include filters that let you sort results by price, cabin class, airline, and departure times, tab view that lets you easily compare your searches, and chart view that lets you see prices across a whole week or month.

Booking.com Hotel – the Booking.com hotel app puts over 612,000 properties at your fingertips. It's not just hotels either – villas, apartments, B & Bs, hostels and more can be booked in over 212 countries worldwide.

Search results can be filtered by price range, city districts, and facilities such as swimming pools, free Wi-Fi, parking, etc. If you also use Booking.com on your computer, you can sign into your account and have your bookings, recent searches, lists, account details and more automatically synced to the app.

National Rail Enquiries – the must-have app for the UK rail traveler, National Rail Enquiries lets you access detailed, real-time train information direct from your iPad. Innovative technology enables you to track specific trains, find out about disruptions to your journey, and re-plan your journey on the go.

Features include progress tracking, departure and arrivals boards for any station, notifications and alerts, ticket prices, London Underground, and much more.

Tripit Travel Organizer – Tripit automatically connects to your email accounts to find travel-confirmation emails, and then turns them into a neat, complete itinerary. TripIt is familiar with purchases you make on all the major search and booking sites, such as Orbitz and Kayak, as well as airlines, car rental services, hotels, restaurant reservations, and more.

cont'd

Weather Live – Weather Live provides you with current weather conditions and forecasts not just for your current location but multiple locations all around the world.

Features include bad weather warnings and alerts, extended forecasts, cloud, satellite and rain maps, and highly configurable options to name just a few. You can also search for a specific location by zipcode, latitude/longitude, IP, airport code, and name.

Currency Converter – an important part of traveling is getting the best conversion rates. Currency Converter is an essential app in this regard and offers live proprietary currency rates, charts, and even stores the last updated rates, so it works when an Internet connection isn't available.

You can monitor up to 10 currencies simultaneously, see over 30,000 currency charts for historic rates, calculate prices with the currency converter, and see live proprietary rates that refresh every minute.

Google Maps – Google Maps is a great app for planning a holiday. The app's driving directions are superb, and its estimates of driving times are very accurate. As a result, it is an excellent tool for planning days out and road trips – it lets you explore different options and zoom in to see what the terrain is like.

You can also use it to take a critical look at places before visiting them. This can be done by switching to the app's satellite and street views.

GPS Navigation – the GPS Navigation app from Telenav GmbH turns your iPad into a fully functional satellite navigation device. It provides turn-by-turn navigation, speed warnings, street sign displays, 3D-view (isometric) and much more.

The traffic information feature keeps you updated on the current traffic situation – this enables you to avoid being caught up in traffic jams and to make detours round construction sites. It can be used to plan suitable routes whether you are a driver, a pedestrian or a cyclist.

Travel List – this handy app lets you put together a list of everything you need and ensures you pack it. As you pack, you tick items off the list, and if you attempt to leave with items still unticked, the app will sound an alarm to alert you.

Travel List comes pre-populated with most items - shirts, t-shirts, dresses, makeup, personal care, gadgets, chargers and so on but you can, of course, add your own items.

Entertainment Apps

The iPad is an excellent device for keeping yourself amused. Apps are available that let you play games, stream movies and TV shows, do crossword puzzles, and much, much more,

Tunein Radio – many people are surprised to find the iPad doesn't come with a radio app. No matter – head over to the App Store and download Tunein Radio. With it, you can listen to over 100,000 radio stations from around the world, including sports, news, talk and music.

Procreate – for the artistically inclined there is Procreate, an incredibly feature-rich painting and drawing app. Providing 120 different brushes, up to 128 layers per image, custom canvas sizes and the ability to create and alter brushes, there are very few limits on what you can create with it.

The app has a slick, smooth interface that's minimalist and easy to learn. Plus, it continuously auto saves, and has Dropbox integration to ensure you never lose your artwork.

Netflix – Netflix is a UK video streaming service that lets you access thousands of movies and television shows for a small monthly fee. A free one month trial is available. However, it has to be said that much of the content has been around for a while now.

Spotify – similar in concept to Netflix, Spotify's forte is music. The app lets you play songs from a library of more than 20 million tracks, build playlists, and get listening recommendations.

Free and premium versions are available. If you decide to pay for a premium account, you get ad-free listening, offline playback, unlimited song skips (instead of the industry-standard six song skips per hour), higher bit-rate streams (320Kbps instead of the standard 128Kbps), and more.

Crosswords Classic – probably the best crossword app of them all, the app gets its content from many different sources including the New York Times, The Onion, The Philadelphia Inquirer, Thinks.com, People Magazine, and many more. This means you get new puzzles every day.

Elevate – rated app of the year, Elevate is a brain training app that lets users train a number of brain faculties, e.g. listening, memory, and comprehension. The app focuses on practical language and math skills such as estimation, comparing values, name recall, as well as reading and listening comprehension.

As with many apps, there are free and premium versions of Elevate, with the premium option providing a better variety of exercises.

CHAPTER 14

Troubleshooting & Maintenance

Your iPad is probably the most reliable computing device you have ever owned. As with all Apple products, it is built to a very high standard. Also, iOS, the operating system that underpins it, is a closed platform open only to Apple itself. This means that, unlike Microsoft's Windows and Google's Android operating systems, it is extremely unlikely to be infected with viruses or to suffer problems introduced by poor quality third-party software.

Having said all that, things will go wrong with your iPad occasionally, although they will usually be minor issues. In this chapter, we examine problems typically experienced on iPads and also the measures you can take to keep yours running smoothly.

Troubleshooting Techniques

Major problems with iPad's are very rare. Most issues you will have with the device are little more than temporary glitches that can usually be fixed in one of the following ways:

Hard Reset – occasionally an iPad will quite literally 'freeze' and refuse to respond to your touch or to the Home button. This is one of those rare major problems we mentioned above. It's easy enough to resolve, though.

Do it by pressing and holding the Power button and the Home button simultaneously. After about 10 seconds, the screen will go black and then turn white showing the Apple logo – at this point, you can release the buttons. After a few more seconds, the Home screen will appear indicating the reset has been successful.

Reboot the iPad – for the multitude of lesser issues that can occur, absolutely the first thing to try is a reboot, i.e. shut the device down and then restart it. This simple action resets internal mechanisms and settings, and will resolve a whole host of problems.

To do it, press and hold the Power button until you see the 'Slide to Power Off' screen. Drag the slider to commence the shut-down procedure – when it is complete the screen will be completely black. Then restart the iPad by holding the Power button down until you see the Apple logo appear on the screen.

Reset the iPad's Settings – there are hundreds of different settings on your iPad and if any of them become corrupt, a malfunction can occur. Assuming a reboot hasn't fixed the problem, the next thing to try is to reset the iPad to its original settings.

Open the Settings app and tap General on the left of the screen. Then scroll down to, and tap, Reset. Finally, tap 'Reset All Settings'. Be aware that while this should resolve the issue, afterwards you will be faced with the task of setting up your iPad again.

This is one very good reason to make a full backup of your device, which you can subsequently use to restore the settings.

Erase and Restore the iPad – if the problem persists after resetting the settings, things are well and truly snarled up and drastic action is called for. Follow the procedure for resetting the iPad's settings but this time tap 'Erase All Content and Settings'.

This will return the iPad to an 'as new' condition with all your settings, apps and data wiped out – which will not really be what you wanted.

However, the problem should also have been wiped out, quite literally. If you've had the foresight to previously make a backup (as you should always do), then you will then be able to restore your settings, apps and data from the backup.

We explained the procedure for doing this in Chapter 11.

Forcibly Close an App – often the problem will not be the iPad itself but rather one of the apps on it. When an app starts misbehaving, simply shut it down and then restart it. This will usually resolve the issue.

The way to do it is to double-press the Home button to launch the multitasking screen. Here, you'll see large images of all the apps open on the iPad. Locate the one that is misbehaving, place your finger on it and swipe upwards. This action will force it to close. Now restart it.

Delete and Reinstall an App – in the very unlikely event of an app still misbehaving after being shut down and restarted, your only option is to delete and then reinstall it.

To do this, press and hold on the app's icon until it starts to jiggle. Then tap the X at the top-left of the icon to delete it and tap the Home button to stop the jiggling. Then go the App Store, locate the app and reinstall it.

Update Your iPad & Apps – your iPad's operating system, iOS, is prone to unforeseen technical issues – this also applies to the apps that run on the iPad. This is one reason that software manufacturers periodically issue updates; these contain patches to fix problems as and when they come to light.

So, if you are experiencing problems, always check to see if there are any updates available for the iPad, or for a specific app, assuming you suspect that's where the problem lies. We explain how to update your iPad on page 210 and your apps on page 73.

Recharge the iPad – forgive us for stating what will be blindingly obvious to most (but not all!) people – an iPad with a flat battery will not work! If your device shows no signs of life, connect it to the charging dock or a computer.

If it immediately powers up and the Apple logo appears after about 20 seconds or so, then all is well – just leave it to charge up completely – you can still use it in the meantime.

Troubleshooting Ancillary Devices

There is a wide range of ancillary devices that can be connected to an iPad to increase its functionality. These include memory sticks, headsets, adaptors of various kinds, battery chargers, speakers, extension keyboards, plus many more.

Inevitably, there will be occasions when one of these devices doesn't work at all, doesn't work properly, or causes the iPad itself to malfunction. As most of the issues likely to occur have already been experienced by someone else and duly documented, it is quite possible that you will find a solution by doing a Google search.

Or, you try the following:

Connections – yes, we know it sounds obvious, but if a device isn't working at all, absolutely the first thing to check is that it is actually connected. If the problem is intermittent, make sure the connection is sound – try wiggling the cable to see if that makes a difference – if it does, there is a loose connection somewhere.

If other devices are part of the setup, make sure these are switched on and connected. For example, if you cannot access the Internet on your iPad, check the router and its connections.

Power Cycling – a very well known (and effective) troubleshooting technique, you power-cycle a device by switching it off, waiting about 10 seconds, and then switching it back on again.

This action resets the device and it is very effective at resolving spurious problems. If the device in question doesn't have an on/off switch, unplug it from the power source or remove its batteries.

Duff Batteries – if a battery-powered device hasn't been used for a while and doesn't work, open the battery compartment and check the batteries for leakage. If they have leaked, there is quite likely to be a poor or broken connection to the terminals. It goes without saying, of course, that the batteries won't be any good anyway.

Default Settings – the device may provide a number of configuration settings that allow you to set it up. Check you haven't inadvertently caused the problem yourself through an incorrect setting – do this by using the device's 'Restore default settings' option – most have one.

Firmware – many devices have a tiny internal program that tells the device what to do, and thus controls it. This is known as firmware, and firmware updates are almost always available from the manufacturer. Check to see if one is available; if so, download and install it.

Extending Battery Life

Batteries have their pros and cons – they allow devices to be portable but there are cost and inconvenience factors involved. So it is always worth extending the life of your batteries as much as possible. With regard to the iPad, these tips will help considerably:

Screen Brightness – your iPad's screen has a voracious appetite for battery power. Reducing its brightness is just about the most effective way to reduce drain on the battery.

Networks – Wi-Fi makes regular checks for the presence of Wi-Fi networks. Similarly, if your iPad is equipped with cellular networking, it will constantly be on the look-out for cellular signals. Bluetooth does the same thing – it is continuously checking for nearby Bluetooth devices. All three types of network place a heavy load on the battery, so turn them off whenever possible.

Mail Check – iPad functions that are constantly active in the background will use battery power constantly. One such function is the Mail app checking the server for new mail. You can restrict the frequency with which it does this by opening the Settings app and tapping Mail, Contacts, Calendars. Ideally, deselect the Push option. If you are using Fetch, in the Fetch section select a longer period or even the Manual option.

Open Apps – the more stuff you have running on your iPad, the more power is needed to keep it all going. Minimize the load placed on the battery by closing all apps that are not being used. Do this by double-tapping the Home button and then swiping upwards on all the apps not in use.

Background App Refresh – apps that use Wi-Fi or mobile networks to update their content make a hit on the battery every time they do so. You can restrict this by going to Settings > General > Background App Refresh. Here, you will see a list of all third-party apps that get content via a network – turn off as many as you can.

To see exactly what percentage of battery power your apps are using, open the Settings app and tap Battery on the left. On the right, you will see a list of recently used apps and the power they have used in the last 24 hours.

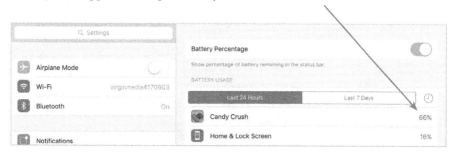

Updating iOS

An important part of keeping any computing device in good working order is to check periodically for software updates. This applies particularly to the device's operating system – iOS on the iPad.

There are two ways to do this: the first is directly from the iPad and the second is with iTunes. Lets start with the iPad method:

1. Open the Settings app and go to General > Software Update

2. Tap Software Update and the iPad will check to see if an update is available. If iOS is up-to-date, you will see a message to this effect

3. If an update is available, you will see a 'Download and Install' link. Tap this and the update will be automatically downloaded and installed

To update your iPad via iTunes:

1. Connect the iPad to your computer and start iTunes

2. In iTunes, click the iPad button at the top-left under the menu bar

3. Click Summary

4. On the right of the screen, click 'Check for Update'. iTunes will connect to Apple's servers to see if an update is available; if there is you will see a description of the update

Given that both methods do the job, why would you choose the more long-winded iTunes method? The answer lies with the available amount of storage space on the iPad, and the fact that iOS updates need to be downloaded fully before they can be installed.

This means that if the iPad doesn't have enough storage space for the download, the installation cannot go ahead. Updating via iTunes, however, will download the update to the computer, which will have sufficient storage space thus eliminating this potential problem.

Wi-Fi Connection Issues

Wireless networking is brilliant when it works but when it doesn't, it can be a real head-scratcher trying to work out the cause. This is compounded by the fact the problem might not even be anything to do with the iPad!

Working through the following checklist will usually help:

Check That Wi-Fi is Switched On – open the Control Center and make sure the Wi-Fi option is on (it is easy to turn this off inadvertently) and that Airplane mode is off.

Connection – is your iPad actually connected to a Wi-Fi network? It is not uncommon for network connections to be dropped for no apparent reason. To check, open the Settings app and, at the top-left, you'll see the name of the network you're connected to. If you don't see it, tap Wi-Fi and then select a network.

Range – Wi-Fi works over very short distances, typically between 150 and 300 feet depending on the network hardware. If your iPad is further than this from the source of the network, i.e. the router, it won't be able to get a strong enough signal.

The obvious solution is to move closer to the router. For a permanent fix, you can install a Wi-Fi range extender or booster.

Interference – interference from nearby electrical gadgets can cause flaky and unreliable Wi-Fi connections. Check to see if there are any devices operating in close proximity and either turn them off or move them further away.

Router – Wi-Fi signals are produced by routers. There are three issues that can affect these devices: first, the device may be faulty; second, it's firmware may need updating; third, the device may need replacing with a more recent model.

With regard to the latter, the 802.11ac Wi-Fi standard is currently the fastest and offers a speed of up to 1733 Mbps.

Router Lease – when your iPad tries to connect to a Wi-Fi network, the router gives it what's known as a 'DHCP lease' – basically, this allows the iPad to access the network. Spurious connectivity issues can often be resolved by renewing this lease.

Open the Settings app and go to Wi-Fi. Tap the blue Information icon at the right of the network you are using, or attempting to use. Make sure you have selected the DHCP tab and then tap Renew Lease.

Managing Storage Space

One of the iPad's limitations is the amount of data it can store – this is particularly so with the 16 GB models. However, the limitation is true of all mobile electronic devices, so until data storage technology comes up with a solution, we all just have to make the best of what's available.

To see just how much storage space you have on your iPad:

1. Open the Settings app

2. Tap General and then tap 'Storage & iCloud Usage'

3. In the Storage section, you'll see exactly how much of your storage space has been used and how much is still available

4. Tap Manage Storage to open a list of all the apps installed on the iPad and see how much storage space each is using

If you need to reclaim some space, one option is to delete an app or two. Do it by tapping on the app and then tapping Delete App in the new screen.

If you wish to avoid having to do this, you need to be careful what you put on the iPad. The worst things for using up your storage space are video of any type and high-resolution pictures.

Index

D

F

E

G

www.ingramcontent.com/pod-product-compliance
Lightning Source LLC
Chambersburg PA
CBHW071114050326
40690CB00008B/1220